Teaching Academic Writing

Center for Teaching Excellence
Brenau University

Jason Brody

Student academic writing is at the heart of teaching and learning in higher education. Students are assessed largely by what they write, and need to learn both general academic conventions as well as disciplinary writing requirements in order to be successful in higher education.

Teaching Academic Writing is a 'toolkit' designed to help higher education lecturers and tutors teach writing to their students. Containing a range of diverse teaching strategies, the book offers both practical activities to help students develop their writing abilities and guidelines to help lecturers and tutors think in more depth about the assessment tasks they set and the feedback they give to students.

The authors explore a wide variety of text types from essays and reflective diaries to research projects and laboratory reports. The book draws on recent research in the fields of academic literacy, second language learning and linguistics. It is grounded in recent developments such as the increasing diversity of the student body, the use of the Internet, electronic tuition, and issues related to distance learning in an era of increasing globalisation.

Written by experienced teachers of writing, language and linguistics, *Teaching Academic Writing* will be of interest to anyone involved in teaching academic writing in higher education.

Caroline Coffin, **Mary Jane Curry**, **Sharon Goodman**, **Ann Hewings**, **Theresa M. Lillis** and **Joan Swann** are all based at the Centre for Language and Communications, The Open University, UK.

Teaching Academic Writing

A toolkit for higher education

Caroline Coffin
Mary Jane Curry
Sharon Goodman
Ann Hewings
Theresa M. Lillis and
Joan Swann

Routledge
Taylor & Francis Group

LONDON AND NEW YORK

First published 2003
by Routledge
11 New Fetter Lane, London EC4P 4EE

Simultaneously published in the USA and Canada
by Routledge
29 West 35th Street, New York, NY 10001

Routledge is an imprint of the Taylor & Francis Group

© 2003 Caroline Coffin, Mary Jane Curry, Sharon Goodman,
Ann Hewings, Theresa M. Lillis and Joan Swann

Typeset in Baskerville by
HWA Text and Data Management, Tunbridge Wells
Printed and bound in Great Britain by
St Edmundsbury Press, Bury St Edmunds, Suffolk

British Library Cataloguing in Publication Data
A catalogue record for this book is available from the British Library

Library of Congress Cataloging in Publication Data
A catalog record for this book has been requested

ISBN 0–415–26135–X (hbk)
ISBN 0–415–26136–8 (pbk)

Contents

List of figures   vii
List of activities   ix
Acknowledgements   xi

1 Issues in academic writing in higher education   **1**

MARY JANE CURRY AND THERESA M. LILLIS

Aims of the book 1
Student writing in a changing higher education context 2
Institutional provision of writing instruction 5
Approaches to student writing 9
What this book offers: a 'toolkit' approach to teaching writing 11
The book's authors 15
Overview of Teaching Academic Writing *15*

2 Approaches to teaching writing   **19**

MARY JANE CURRY AND ANN HEWINGS

Introduction 19
The purposes of writing 20
Teaching writing: focus on text 21
Teaching writing: focus on process 32
Integrating the process approach with text analysis 43
Conclusion 44

3 Writing for different disciplines   **45**

CAROLINE COFFIN AND ANN HEWINGS

Introduction 45
Sciences to the humanities: academic knowledge as a continuum 47

Writing project proposals and experimental reports: examples from science 49
Representing data and discipline-specific terminology:
  examples from the social sciences 52
Writing an essay: an example from the humanities 57
Writing a case study: an example from business studies 66
Conclusion 71

4 Planning the assessment of student writing 73

SHARON GOODMAN AND JOAN SWANN

Introduction 73
Assessment: preliminary issues 74
Identifying what types of writing to assess 81
The wording of assignments 89
Students' participation in assessment 92
Pre-empting plagiarism 95
Conclusion 100

5 Giving feedback on student writing 101

THERESA M. LILLIS AND JOAN SWANN

Introduction 101
Institutional demands and research insights 102
Identifying the purposes of feedback 104
Commenting on students' writing 105
Ways of communicating feedback 111
Developing 'feedback dialogues' 121
Conclusion 128

6 Academic writing in an electronic environment 130

CAROLINE COFFIN AND SHARON GOODMAN

Introduction 130
Internet-based resources 134
Using electronic conferencing to develop students' academic writing 141
Technology and assessment 153
Conclusion 156

Annotated bibliography 158
References 163
Index 170

Figures

2.1 Two typical text types and their functional organisation   22
2.2 Signposting conjunctions   24
2.3 Patterns of spelling error   31
2.4 The apostrophe   32
2.5 Some common grammatical errors in student writing   33
2.6 The writing process approach   34
2.7 Brainstorm on 'issues related to immigration'   35
2.8 Cluster diagram on issues of immigration   38
2.9 Outline on the economic benefits of immigration   39
3.1 A categorisation of disciplines and their typical written texts   46
3.2 The academic knowledge continuum   48
3.3 Tips for writing reports on scientific experiments   51
3.4 Comparing similar texts   52
3.5 Guidance on using illustrative material   54
3.6 Three ways of structuring an argument essay   60
3.7 Arguments and evidence in an abridged history essay   62
3.8 A continuum of less endorsing to more endorsing terms
     for referring to sources   66
3.9 The functional stages of a case study   69
4.1 Marking criteria on an English language course   78
4.2 Grade-related criteria on a literature course   79
4.3 Weighted criteria from a business studies course   80
4.4 Some alternatives to the essay and the laboratory report   82
4.5 'Concept essays' from a course on calculus   82
4.6 Students' responses to the assessment of reflective writing   84
4.7 Extracts from journal entries completed by dentistry
     students   85

4.8	Collaborative writing produced for assessment	87
4.9	Common assignment key words	90
4.10	A problem with question wording	92
4.11	Taking account of peer comments in assessment	94
4.12	Checklist for students to use as part of self-assessment	96
4.13	How to avoid accidental plagiarism	98
4.14	How to recognise unacceptable and acceptable paraphrases	98
4.15	Plagiarism resulting from clumsy paraphrasing	99
5.1	Some common errors in student writing	108
5.2	Spoken feedback	113
5.3	Feedback proforma	114
5.4	Extract from open-ended comments on a student's essay	114
5.5	Strengths and limitations of structured feedback proformas and open-ended comments	116
5.6	Open-ended feedback	117
5.7	Student text with tutor commentary	120
5.8	Student text with numbered comment	120
5.9	Guidance to students on how to use feedback	121
5.10	Sheet 1: Students comment on their writing	123
5.11	Sheet 2: Students assess their writing	125
5.12	Extended feedback dialogue	126
5.13	A student's account of taking responsibility for her writing	127
6.1	Student writing and technology: a map of resources	131
6.2	Glossary of computer terms	132
6.3	Sample desktop screen from an electronic conference	135
6.4	Sub-conference showing individual messages and discussion threads	136
6.5	Extract from a downloadable handout on Purdue University's OWL	138
6.6	Sample messages from Academic Writing On-line course	139
6.7	Evaluating websites	140
6.8	Strategies for creating an on-line community	142
6.9	Modelling an informal style	144
6.10	Model text illustrating effective electronic conferencing	145
6.11	Developing academic argument in an electronic conference	146
6.12	Activity from MA in Open and Distance Education H805, Open University	147

Activities

2.1 An introduction to the purposes of writing   20
2.2 Argument and academic writing   26
2.3 Formality in writing   29
2.4 The use of personal voice in academic writing   30
2.5 Student guidelines for peer review   41
3.1 Functional stages of the scientific project proposal   50
3.2 Tutorial examining the use of a graph   55
3.3 Defining and classifying using discipline-specific language   56
3.4 What makes an argument essay persuasive?   58
3.5 Developing a stance on evidence   64
3.6 Comparing student voices   70
4.1 Considering the requirements of an assignment   83
5.1 Giving feedback   105
5.2 Making sense of feedback   107
5.3 Formal and informal language in academic writing   110
5.4 Some uses of first-person forms in academic writing   111
5.5 Feedback dialogues   126
6.1 Establishing ground rules for conferencing   143
6.2 Comparing forms of academic argument   150

Acknowledgements

We would like to offer our grateful thanks to the following reviewers of earlier drafts of this book: Maria Graal, Dorothy Faulkner, Iain Garner, Mary R. Lea and Verina Waights.

Thanks also to Sarah P. North for the illustrations in Chapter 2 and to David Hewings for redrawing the graph in Activity 3.2. Finally, our gratitude to Pam Burns and Elaine Ware for their secretarial support.

Grateful acknowledgement for permission to reprint is extended for: Extract from T. Dudley-Evans, *Writing Laboratory Reports*, Melbourne: Thomas Nelson. Sample HSC Answers Modern History © Board of Studies NSW, 1991. Material reproduced by permission of Oxford University Press Australia from *Communicating in Geography and the Environmental Sciences* by Iain Hay, © Oxford University Press, www.oup.com.au. Extract from Alison Wray (1996) 'The occurrence of "occurance"', in G.M. Blue and R. Mitchell (eds) *Language and Education*. Papers from the Annual Meeting of the British Association for Applied Linguistics held at the University of Southampton, September 1995 (pp. 94–106). Clevedon: Multilingual Matters. Extract from J. Pieterick, *Writing for Academic Success*, Module Guide FD1000a (SLS), University of Wolverhampton. Extract from 'How to recognize unacceptable and acceptable paraphrases' from the Indiana University Campus Writing Program. For the punctuation sheet from M. Harris (1986) *Teaching One-to-One: The Writing Conference*, copyright © 1986 by the National Council of Teachers of English. Reprinted with permission. For extract from appendix reprinted from *English for Specific Purposes*, Vol. 18, R. Tang and S. John, 'The "I" in identity: exploring writer identity in student academic writing through the first person pronoun', pp. S23–S39, copyright 1999, with permission from Elsevier Science. Extract adapted from G. Salmon (2000) *E-moderating: The Key to Teaching and Learning Online*, London: Kogan Page. For 'Active/Passive Voice' from the Purdue University website entitled 'On-Line Writing Lab (OWL)', PRF Ref. No. C-0096. Student checklist from D. Hounsell (1995) 'Marking and commenting on essays', in F. Forster, D. Hounsell and S. Thompson (eds) *Tutoring and Demonstrating: A Handbook*, Centre for Teaching, Learning, and Assessment, Department of Higher and Further Education, University of Edinburgh. From D. Ferris and J.S. Hedgcock (1998) *Teaching ESL Composition: Purpose, Process, and Practice*, Mahwah, NJ: Lawrence Erlbaum. Glossary of computer terms from the Open University website http://www.open.ac.uk/learning/tutor-resources/tutor/cmcpdf/cmctk_a.pdf.

Chapter 1

Issues in academic writing in higher education

AIMS OF THE BOOK

Teaching Academic Writing is an introductory book on the teaching of academic writing in higher education. It is aimed at higher education lecturers and writing tutors who wish to help undergraduates improve their academic writing in both discipline-specific and writing/study skills contexts. The book raises issues about the teaching of academic writing and offers many practical suggestions about how academic writing can be taught. Some suggestions are meant for lecturers to implement as part of their subject teaching; other ideas will work better in collaboration with writing or language specialists who work alongside subject specialists to help students with their writing. The book will also be useful for people who work in contexts where writing support is offered as a separate provision, for example within study skills and EAP courses (English for academic purposes). Whilst the book is aimed principally at lecturers and tutors working with undergraduate students, it raises many issues which are relevant to those who teach postgraduate students, particularly those students who are returning to higher education after a break from academic study.[1] The aims of the book are:

- to identify and demystify the conventions and practices associated with academic writing so that both subject specialists and writing support staff can better advise and help students to construct their written work
- to discuss ways that lecturers can address the needs of a variety of students, including those with little experience in academic writing and those whose primary language is not English

- to enable lecturers in a range of contexts to adopt and adapt various teaching strategies to the teaching of academic writing for different purposes
- to combine a practical orientation to teaching writing with a grounding in current theories of writing instruction.

STUDENT WRITING IN A CHANGING HIGHER EDUCATION CONTEXT

Student writing is at the centre of teaching and learning in higher education, fulfilling a range of purposes according to the various contexts in which it occurs. These purposes include:

- *assessment*, which is often a major purpose for student writing (see National Committee of Inquiry into Higher Education, 1997). Students may be required to produce essays, written examinations, or laboratory reports whose main purpose is to demonstrate their mastery of disciplinary course content. In assessing such writing, lecturers focus on both the content and the form of the writing, that is the language used, the text structure, the construction of argument, grammar and punctuation.
- *learning*, which can help students grapple with disciplinary knowledge as well as develop more general abilities to reason and critique (Hilgers *et al.*, 1999). Separately from or simultaneously with writing for assessment, students may also be asked to write texts that trace their reflections on the learning process itself, as with journals where they record thoughts, questions, problems, and ideas about readings, lectures, and applied practice.
- *entering particular disciplinary communities*, whose communication norms are the primary means by which academics transmit and evaluate ideas (Prior, 1998). As they progress through the university, students are often expected to produce texts that increasingly approximate the norms and conventions of their chosen disciplines, with this expectation peaking at the level of postgraduate study.

Students and lecturers alike recognise the necessity for good communication skills both within the university and in the larger world. Whilst some research signals that an ever-increasing range of writing demands are being made of students (Ganobcsik-Williams, 2001), evidence also indicates that the most traditional of practices – that of essay writing – continues to hold sway across many disciplines (see National Committee of Inquiry into Higher Education, 1997). Whether the essay should continue to be the main type of writing that students produce and whether students know how to successfully engage in this and other writing practices are questions being voiced more and more frequently.[2] In this book, whilst our main focus is on essay writing, we also deal with other kinds of writing such as laboratory reports, project reports, case studies, and reflective journals.

Student academic writing continues to be at the centre of teaching and learning in higher education, but is often an invisible dimension of the curriculum; that is, the rules or conventions governing what counts as academic writing are often assumed to be part of the 'common sense' knowledge students have, and are thus not explicitly taught within disciplinary courses. If students lack familiarity with these conventions, the assumption is often held that they will 'pick it up' as part of learning their subject knowledge. Although this position might have been understandable within the context of a small and predominantly homogenous higher education system, it is no longer justified within current contexts where significant changes are affecting all aspects of teaching and learning, including student academic writing. These changes include:

Increasing student numbers. The growth of student participation in higher education signals a shift away from a small, highly elitist provision of higher education toward policies and practices aimed at widening access to more of the population. In the UK at the end of the 1930s only some 2 per cent of the population took part in higher education, compared with some 10 per cent in the 1960s and some 30 per cent by the late 1990s. The UK government plans to increase this proportion to up to 50 per cent of the 18- to 30-year-old population by the year 2005 (HEFCE, 2001). Policies of widening participation have been a driving force behind a heightened interest in teaching and learning, including student writing, in many parts of the world. The growing UK interest in teaching writing thus mirrors trends in South Africa, Australia, and the United States.

Increasing diversity of the student population. The student population is not only larger and still growing but significantly more diverse than previous generations of students. Increasing numbers of 'non-traditional' students, that is, students from social groups historically excluded from higher education, are now present. These include students from working-class backgrounds, those who are older than 18 when they start university, and students from a wide range of cultural and linguistic backgrounds (HEFCE, 2001). There are also large numbers of international students who have been mainly educated in countries other than the UK. Educational background, ethnicity, cultural expectations and gender all influence how students read academic texts and respond in writing (Lillis, 2001). Students new to higher education may not feel at ease with academic writing conventions or with staking claims for knowledge about which their lecturers have greater expertise, necessitating more explicit instruction about writing.

Complex patterns of participation in higher education. There are complex patterns of participation including greater numbers of part-time students in higher education, in contrast to the traditional, full-time model. In the UK, part-time participation has been steadily on the increase and has been taken up particularly by women (see Blackburn and Jarman, 1993; HEFCE, 2001; Ramsden, 2001).

Curriculum changes. There have been significant curriculum changes, not least in shifts towards modularisation and interdisciplinarity. Modularisation, whereby teaching and learning are structured around short courses rather than over a whole academic year, has grown substantially in the past ten years. By 1994 it was estimated that more than half of UK universities had moved to semester provision, which was linked in many cases to modularisation of the curriculum and delivery (Schuller, 1995). Interdisciplinarity, whereby a growing number of courses offer modules in a wide range of subject areas, happens within particular interdisciplinary degrees such as communication studies and women's studies, but also in routes through more traditionally demarcated subject areas. There has also been growth in vocationally and professionally oriented higher education courses that cross academic boundaries, for example, nursing and social work studies.

Diverse modes of curriculum delivery. The introduction of a range of modes of curriculum 'delivery' has been profoundly shaped by developments in information technology. The most notable shift has been away from conventional face-to-face teaching and learning modes and toward the use of computer conferencing systems and web-based materials, both as part of campus-based provision and increasingly in distance courses.

The impact of such changes on traditional practices of teaching, learning and assessment is only just beginning to be explored (see e.g. Richardson, 2000).

Contexts for teaching and learning. The increase in student numbers has not been matched by an equivalent increase in funding. Many institutions have larger class sizes, fewer opportunities for small group teaching (such as seminars and tutorials) and – of specific relevance to student writing – little time for lecturers to comment on students' written work. Whilst the nature of the material conditions for teaching and learning varies immensely across institutions, a notable difference frequently emerges between the 'old' and 'new' universities.[3] The 'new' universities often have larger classes compared with 'old' universities such as the prestigious institutions of Oxford and Cambridge, where a highly personalised teaching and learning context prevails in the form of the tutorial system. Nonetheless, many innovations in pedagogy are taking place at new universities in response to these changing contexts and at national levels in many parts of the world there is unprecedented interest in teaching and learning in higher education. In the UK the recent establishment of the Institute for Learning and Teaching (ILT) placed teaching in higher education firmly on the political agenda, thus mirroring current and historical developments in similar contexts elsewhere. (For a current parallel, see the white paper on higher education in South Africa at http://196.14.128.104/Deptinfo/highereduc/hewp1.html; for historically similar developments in the United States, see Crowley, 1999; Horner and Lu, 1999.)

This book's focus on the teaching of academic writing is therefore part of a current interest in teaching and learning in higher education more generally. Questions, and possible answers, about how best to support students' academic writing are relevant to all those committed to enhancing successful teaching and learning in higher education.

INSTITUTIONAL PROVISION OF WRITING INSTRUCTION

A range of approaches to teaching writing has developed in different geographical contexts and for different historical and socio-political reasons. In Australia, pedagogical models designed to foster students' awareness of academic conventions and practices have emerged from the study of disciplinary genres and the field of systemic functional linguistics (see e.g. Martin and Veel, 1998). In the United States, for decades courses in 'freshman composition' have taught the presumed generic skills of academic writing to first-year students as well as non-native speakers of English (Leki, 2001; Zamel and Spack, 1998). Recently interest has grown in teaching writing in the disciplines or across the curriculum, in recognition of the discipline-specific nature of much of academic writing and the usefulness of writing to the learning process. In South Africa, where fundamental changes in higher education are taking place, teachers and researchers are critically reconceptualising the purpose and nature of student writing in the academy (see e.g. Angelil-Carter, 1998; Thesen, 2001).

Institutional structures around the world tend to include any of four main locations for the teaching of writing: dedicated writing courses, disciplinary subject courses, English for academic purposes/English for speakers of other languages departments, and study skills or writing centres. In addition to these face-to-face venues, on-line writing instruction has recently added another dimension – or at least the possibility for it – to all of these domains.

Dedicated writing courses

First-year writing, or 'freshman composition', is usually a required course at the beginning of university study in the United States. Depending on university policy, first-year students may take remedial/basic writing courses, freshman composition, or more advanced writing courses. As the provision of writing instruction has increased, higher level courses in academic writing have been developed. In some cases these courses link disciplinary lecturers with writing specialists to focus on disciplinary forms of writing, as in 'learning communities' (Grubb, 1999). The development of the academic field of composition studies in the United States in the past 35 years came about partly as a response to increased numbers of non-traditional students entering the academy. Veterans of the Second World War, greater numbers of racial and ethnic minorities, women, and disabled students all changed the face of the student population in higher education. The needs of these students to acquire academic literacy functioned to expose some of the hidden assumptions and practices of the academy. The growth of composition studies also came from increased attention to theories of teaching and learning writing. For many of the same reasons, UK universities have also recently begun to provide courses dedicated to teaching academic writing.

Disciplinary subject courses

With the increasing recognition of the centrality of writing to learning and assessment in higher education, the movement to include writing across the curriculum (WAC) and writing in the disciplines (WID) has grown (see e.g. Bazerman and Russell, 1994; Fulwiler, 1986). The WAC movement is premised not only on the notion that writing is a tool for learning but also that because academic writing happens in specific disciplinary contexts, instruction in such writing should also be located in these courses. One benefit of incorporating writing in the disciplines is that students can see how different forms of writing occur in different contexts. WAC/WID pedagogy also emphasises the sequencing of writing tasks throughout a course so that students build gradually into particular forms of writing.

Study support centres and writing centres

Within many higher education institutions, writing instruction has often been located in departments or centres that offer support in study skills. Because such centres are frequently situated outside academic departments, study skills specialists have offered the 'service' of helping students with their written work. In many cases these services are provided to students referred to study skills centres because their lecturers deem their work to be deficient. Like EAP lecturers (see below), study skills specialists may have little subject-area knowledge; they may also not have much communication with the lecturers who set writing assignments, provide feedback, and assess students' written work.

Writing centres have often evolved from study skills centres. In some cases, writing centres have assumed a higher-status role as their functions have broadened to encompass offering mini-courses on specific aspects of academic and other types of writing. The most recent development in writing centres has been the addition of on-line writing support (see below).

English for academic purposes

A large number of non-traditional students in higher education are international students and other non-native speakers of English. To cater for their needs, academics in the fields of ESOL (English for speakers of other languages) and EAP have often combined writing instruction with language teaching and learning. The experiences, backgrounds, and needs of non-native English speakers vary considerably. Immigrant or 'home' students may have different English language learning and writing experiences than those of international students studying in the UK and other English-speaking countries. ESOL/EAP lecturers who teach second language writing often have been trained in applied linguistics or language teaching; thus their expertise may be in different subject areas than those of their students. Many, however, work together with subject lecturers or make themselves familiar with the writing needs of their students (Graal and Clark, 2000; Johns and Dudley-Evans, 1981). As a result non-native speakers of English often obtain much of their knowledge about academic literacy in Western universities from their EAP courses. The knowledge of different academic text types and disciplinary variation is less frequently shared with 'home' students, who may not take such courses.

Writing on-line

The on-line teaching of writing covers a range of activities, from electronic mail to websites to synchronous and asynchronous conferencing, as Chapter 6 discusses. Electronic mail can be used to maintain communication between lecturers and students as well as among students on a course, as a venue for student journals, and as a means of transferring student texts to the lecturer or peer readers. Websites connected to writing centres offer round-the-clock access to writing guides, style manuals, course materials, and in some cases, feedback from writing specialists. The most interactive forms of electronic communication are conferencing systems that allow students to post their texts in public and engage in public dialogues with other students and the course lecturer.

The range of institutional provision outlined above has developed in response to local circumstances and contexts. What these structures share is an assumption that students should be taught how to improve their academic writing. Exactly what constitutes such teaching varies. In some contexts writing or study skills tutors work with individual students; in other settings tutors work as partners with subject lecturers in order to integrate approaches to the teaching of writing within the teaching of discipline-specific content areas. Throughout the book we suggest ways in which such tutors and lecturers can work to support students' writing.

APPROACHES TO STUDENT WRITING

Exactly how individual tutors support students' writing varies across, and indeed within, the range of institutional provision outlined in the previous section. However, there are three influential approaches to the teaching of student writing that it is useful to consider. We refer to these approaches in the following way: *writing as text, writing as process* and *writing as social practice*. Such approaches have developed over time and often in distinct geographical contexts but to a greater or lesser extent they inform how writing is currently being taught.

Text approaches

Historically, when writing has been explicitly taught in higher education, the emphasis has been on students' writing as final texts or 'products'. Teaching writing – whether in formal writing classes or as an activity within discipline-based courses – often entailed presenting students with 'models of good writing', and asking them to imitate these exemplars. Often, little analysis occurred of the various rhetorical aspects of the texts or the social contexts in which the texts functioned. The focus instead was on specific features of the written texts, for example, spelling, text structure, vocabulary, style. In addition, little attention was typically paid to the process of writing, including the conscious and unconscious decisions that writers make in order to communicate for different purposes and to different audiences. In an era in which students may have been more homogenous and shared previous educational experiences and social backgrounds, the assumption was again often made that students could pick up how to do academic writing through this process of imitation.

More recent textual approaches to writing have focused on genres, or text types, such as essays, and project and laboratory reports. These are identified and explicitly analysed with students.[4] Such a discussion often includes larger dimensions of writing such as the rhetorical purposes of particular text types within disciplines and the relationship between author and audience, or more local concerns such as how to set out a discussion of results in a report on an experiment. The move toward making explicit to students the requirements of different text types has highlighted how apparently universal text types such as the essay vary in purpose or function and in different disciplines.

Process approaches

Attention in process approaches to writing is paid to the steps and stages of writing that an individual writer might work through. Process writing emerged from the individualist, expressivist impulse popular throughout education in the 1960s and 1970s, and parts of it retain much currency today. Following the notion of the discrete, isolated individual, the emphasis in process writing was chiefly on how students could express their identities, rather than on writing as something that occurs in a social context. Critics of process approaches (see e.g. Delpit, 1995) have argued that explicit teaching of the forms and conventions of academic writing must accompany any focus on process in order for students to gain control of dominant academic forms.

Writing as a social practice

Here the focus is on writing as an activity that always occurs in a social context, at both a more local, immediate level and at a broader social and cultural level. In the context of higher education, there are different ways in which student writing can be understood as a 'social practice'. First, student writing is always embedded within relationships around teaching and learning and these relationships influence, not least, the extent to which students come to write successfully in higher education. Second, the conventions governing exactly what constitutes 'appropriate academic writing' are social to the extent that these have developed within specific academic and disciplinary communities over time. Third, student academic writing is a social practice in that the writers, students, are learning not only to communicate in particular ways, but are learning how to 'be' particular kinds of people: that is, to write 'as academics', 'as geographers', 'as social scientists'. Thus academic writing is also about personal and social identity. Some students may find it harder or less comfortable to take on these identities than others. This focus on identity in academic writing has been emphasised in recent times; educational background, ethnicity, cultural expectations and gender have all been shown to influence how students read academic texts and respond in writing (Ivanic, 1998; Lillis, 2001).

In offering ideas for teaching student writing in this book, we draw on elements from all of these approaches, with some chapters focusing more closely on some approaches than others. Chapter 2 discusses the writing process and some generic features of student academic writing. Chapter 3 offers a textual approach focusing on a linguistic analysis of text types. Chapters 4 and 5 take a broader perspective by examining key moments of student writing within higher education: assessment and feedback. Chapter 6 addresses key issues arising out of the growing use of information technology in teaching writing.

WHAT THIS BOOK OFFERS: A 'TOOLKIT' APPROACH TO TEACHING WRITING

In calling this book 'a toolkit' to teaching writing, we are using the term 'toolkit' in two ways: first to signal our theoretical stance on language and learning, and second to indicate that our main purpose is to provide a range of practical ideas for teaching student writing – and reflecting on the purposes of such writing – in higher education.

Language as a cultural toolkit for learning

Our approach to writing involves a theory of language and learning which can be broadly referred to as 'sociocultural'. This means that rather than viewing language as a system of signs or symbols independent of social context, we view language as a culturally shaped resource for making meaning. Language within this frame refers not just to words and sentences (if we're thinking about written language) in isolation, but to the ways in which such words have come to be used and the social conventions governing their use. Language as a cultural resource that we all use can, to a certain extent, usefully be conceptualised as a number of tools or as a toolkit that we draw on to make meaning in different contexts, in different ways (see Wertsch, 1991). Whilst it is potentially vast, language-as-toolkit is not the same for all users. Individuals gain access to particular ways of using language through participating in the specific social and cultural contexts where certain types of language are required. Learning to use new ways with words in new or different contexts may be very exciting but it can also be difficult or even frightening.

In higher education, particular ways of using language have become associated with, and valued in, student academic writing: these are ways with words, particular ways of constructing meanings – some to do with the histories of academic disciplines (e.g. history, physics, linguistics) and some more broadly with the traditions and conventions of Western academia – and ways of organising written texts. To introduce students to these different aspects of language use, our view is that as lecturers and writing tutors we need to do the following: a) identify the kinds of language use with which students need to become familiar in order to write successfully in higher education; b) make these uses available to students in ways which enhance their learning and motivation for writing and participating in higher education; and c) find ways of building on students' existing knowledge of and uses of language.

These last points, above, signal our understanding of what constitutes successful teaching and learning. Briefly, following Vygotsky and neo-Vygotskian research, we conceptualise successful teaching and learning as a 'scaffolded' activity, whereby lecturers actively support and guide students' participation in knowledge-making practices (Bruner, 1983; Vygotsky, 1978). In the process of scaffolding, a more advanced 'expert' or 'teacher' is seen as helping a less-experienced student to learn to do a particular task so that the learner can replicate the process alone at some point in the future. For successful scaffolding to take place, lecturers need to know where the student is starting from and aiming for in the process of learning. A key aspect of this scaffolding activity in the teaching of student writing is raising students' awareness of the conventions within which they are expected to write and then helping students to add these conventions to their linguistic and rhetorical repertoires.

Tools for teaching writing

We also use the notion of a toolkit approach at a more concrete level to indicate what we are offering in this book: a range of tools, or ideas for thinking about and teaching student writing in higher education. In constructing this toolkit, we draw on a considerable body of research from the traditions referred to earlier. Our decision to explore what each of these has to offer, rather than argue that one approach or one tool can suit all purposes, stems from our acknowledgement of the varied and complex contexts in which lecturers and students are working in higher education and the range of experiences and expertise of all involved. The kinds of tools we use in the book are of two main types:

> *Heuristics* – sets of questions for thinking about what's going on in student texts and what kind of response or feedback might be most appropriate at a particular moment, or to encourage reflection on different aspects of teaching writing. These questions are set apart from the discussion with lines above and below them.
> *Activities* – specific suggestions for lecturers and tutors to use either with students or in responding to student writing. These are labelled as Activities throughout the book, and sometimes function with the reflection questions.

The terminology in this book

When discussing students' written texts in this book, we use frameworks and terminology that are widely used by subject lecturers and writing support tutors, as well as some more specialist linguistic terminology. We have attempted to keep specialist linguistic terminology to a minimum, but we have found it useful in discussing various aspects of the teaching and learning of student writing to include some terminology, which may be new to some readers. Below we give an overview of the key terms we use, which are further defined and exemplified in relevant sections of the book. When other specialist terms are introduced throughout the book, you will find the first mention of a term in italics followed by a brief definition.

At an overarching level we have distinguished between two kinds of approaches to students' written texts: what we call 'a focus on linguistic accuracy' and 'a focus on text types'. Linguistic accuracy includes aspects such as spelling, punctuation and grammatical accuracy. By 'grammatical accuracy' we mean things like subject-verb agreement (i.e. *she works*, rather than *she work*), consistent use of verb tenses, and writing in complete sentences using appropriate punctuation. Many comments on students' texts refer to these different aspects of linguistic accuracy. Although we recognise that such conventions shift over time, they are an important aspect of creating shared meaning.

It is also important to think of students' writing in terms of what we call *text types*. Typical academic text types include essays, laboratory reports, research projects reports, and reflective diaries. Whilst the exact nature of these text types varies according to disciplines, departmental practices and the preferences of individual lecturers, it is useful to consider what these text types broadly involve. In this book we foreground three key dimensions of text types: *rhetorical purpose*, *register* and *text structure*, all of which can be explicitly discussed with students both when setting assignments and when commenting on their writing. By *rhetorical purpose* we mean the overt communicative purpose of the text. So, for example, the overt rhetorical purpose of the essay is to construct an argument, whereas the main rhetorical purpose of the laboratory report is to provide an account of a scientific procedure, giving specific information in a predetermined format. Whilst the rhetorical purpose of any text may be far less straightforward than we might often assume – for example, argument means many different things in different contexts – we think it is useful to discuss the rhetorical purpose of writing tasks with students. Argument is considered to be the key rhetorical purpose of much academic writing, indeed is seen as an essential aspect of intellectual activity within higher education. For this reason we focus on argument in several chapters in the book: in Chapter 2 we focus on academic argument in general terms and in Chapter 3 we discuss some discipline-specific aspects of argument.

By *register* we mean the vocabulary and sentence structures which students are expected to use in written texts. Some lecturers and tutors may refer to this as 'style'. Academic writing involves much specialist vocabulary and particular kinds of sentence structures. Some of these are general features of academic writing and some are discipline-specific. Thus, for example, academic vocabulary and sentence structure are generally considered to be more formal than many other types of communication, and seem to be what students mean when they talk about having to use 'long words' in their writing. These general aspects of academic language are discussed in Chapter 2; some discipline-specific issues surrounding language are discussed in Chapter 3. Throughout the book we argue that aspects of register should be explicitly explored with students.

By *text structure* we mean the ways in which complete texts are structured and form a coherent whole. Often text structures are discussed with students as if these were quite unproblematic – for example, 'in an essay, you need an introduction, a main part and a conclusion'. However, as Chapters 2 and 3 discuss, there are more specific ways of analysing the organisation of texts with students which can help them improve their academic writing.

THE BOOK'S AUTHORS

Separately and together, the six authors of *Teaching Academic Writing* have many years of experience teaching and researching academic writing. We have taught in distance and face-to-face settings, including the Open University in the United Kingdom and traditional universities and colleges of further education in countries including Costa Rica, Italy, Malaysia, the United Kingdom, the United States, and Australia. We have worked in settings ranging from secondary to undergraduate to adult education to postgraduate programmes in English education and applied linguistics. We have taught both native and non-native speakers of English who have a variety of backgrounds. Our research has included looking at our own teaching practice as well as the experiences of students and lecturers working in other classrooms and institutions. Our sometimes – but not always – complementary and overlapping approaches and theoretical frameworks include writing as social practice, process writing approaches, and systemic functional linguistics.

OVERVIEW OF *TEACHING ACADEMIC WRITING*

The remaining five chapters of the book focus on broad issues related to student writing and the challenges facing lecturers in terms of introducing students to the writing conventions relevant to their disciplines, setting assignments, assessing student work, and using electronic communication to teach writing. In addition to discussing its main topic, each chapter includes Activities for teaching and doing academic writing. Throughout the book we use authentic examples from student writing. Where these have appeared in publications, we reference the sources. In other cases, we draw on our research projects, for which we have received students' permission to cite their texts. We have tried to write these chapters so that they can largely be read on their own but we do refer readers to related issues discussed in other chapters. At the end of the book we offer an annotated bibliography of selected books and papers which we consider to be particularly useful, which stands apart from the references that we cite in each chapter.

Chapter 2, 'Approaches to teaching writing', focuses on academic writing at a general level. It explores issues of general concern and offers practical approaches to the teaching of writing which can be used in both study/writing support sessions and within disciplinary contexts. It considers various ways in which 'argument' is understood and used in academic writing and discusses issues related to teaching students to construct different text types, use evidence, and draw on sources. It provides suggestions for students to develop awareness of the norms of the various text types they encounter in different disciplines. The chapter also covers various techniques for teaching writing processes, including prewriting activities, student journals, the stages of drafting an essay, and peer review.

Chapter 3, 'Writing for different disciplines', looks at the implications for student writing of the requirements of various disciplines. It identifies major text types and aspects of writing in four broad disciplinary areas: the sciences, the social sciences, humanities and arts, and the applied disciplines such as business and education. It explores ways of initiating students into appreciating the 'constructedness' of specific text types and their disciplinary differences, for example, the way in which different disciplines base their arguments on different types of evidence. The chapter emphasises ways in which discipline specialists can help students to become aware of academic writing requirements – both those that operate across disciplinary boundaries and those that are shaped by specific disciplinary paradigms and conventions.

Chapter 4, 'Planning the assessment of student writing', focuses on issues related to the design and assessment of writing assignments. Assessment practices vary across subjects and academic areas, as well as between individual lecturers, and requirements are not always made clear to students. Miscommunication between students and lecturers can result from factors including students' unfamiliarity with the conventions of academic assessment; their experiences of differing assessment practices between courses and between lecturers; differing cultural expectations; and differing language backgrounds. An important and problematic assessment issue that lecturers regularly face is plagiarism. The rise of the Internet has engendered ever-more sophisticated and widespread techniques of plagiarism. Yet what lecturers perceive as 'cheating' may stem from students' lack of understanding of academic writing conventions, differing cultural models for citing experts, the results of collaborative learning, or students' failure to reference adequately. Chapter 4 problematises the concept of plagiarism and offers suggestions for tackling it at different points in the assessment process.

Chapter 5, 'Giving feedback on student writing', addresses an important component of teaching writing. Higher education lecturers spend much time and energy in providing feedback to students on their writing. Feedback, whether written or spoken, is crucial in these ways: it can justify and explain marks awarded for a piece of writing; it can highlight the academic conventions within which students are expected to write; and it can suggest ways for students to improve their future writing. Given the range of purposes for providing feedback, it is important to understand which kinds of feedback practices are useful. Whilst much feedback is given, it may often be of little relevance to students, particularly to those least familiar with academic writing practices. Chapter 5 illustrates why widely used feedback practices often cause confusion rather than fulfilling lecturers' aims of teaching students academic writing, and discusses ways in which feedback practices can offer students greater support.

Chapter 6, 'Academic writing in an electronic environment', focuses on the increasing use of electronic communication for teaching and learning writing in both local and distance contexts. Electronic tuition raises important issues related to forms of writing. Chapter 6 discusses the possibilities created by information technology for teaching and learning academic writing. The spectrum covered ranges from electronic mail at one end of technological interaction, to course websites and on-line conferencing at the other end.

NOTES

1 Throughout the book we use the term 'lecturer' to refer to teachers in higher education who are responsible for teaching a discipline area, and 'tutor' to refer to teachers who are responsible for writing, language or study skill support.
2 This debate is evident in developments such as funded projects on key skills in higher education, one of which is 'communication'; the growth of discussion groups on writing in higher education in the UK, relating to both research and pedagogy; and conferences and research groups on academic literacies (e.g. the Writing Development in Higher Education conferences, the Academic Literacies group at the Institute of Education, London).

3 'New' universities in the UK are those which before 1992 were polytechnics but which since then can claim university status.

4 We use text type throughout the book to indicate that our principal focus is on the key text types – and their component parts – that students are asked to write in higher education. We have chosen not to use the word 'genre' because of the debates surrounding the meaning of this term within applied linguistics, a discussion of which is not central to our aims in the book.

Chapter 2

Approaches to teaching writing

The lecturer's dilemma

Iain, a psychology lecturer, became interested in the role of writing in his students' learning for 'selfish reasons'. When reading his students' writing, Iain found it difficult to distinguish between their understanding of the subject matter and their expression of ideas and arguments. This problem drove him to investigate how to improve his students' academic writing abilities. A key issue that he identified was the need for students to be able to argue and defend positions in the field of psychology in their writing. Currently, Iain and other lecturers in his department are working to build academic writing instruction into the structure of their psychology courses.

INTRODUCTION

At the university level, disciplinary knowledge and understanding are largely exhibited and valued through the medium of writing. Students can begin to understand the significance of writing by becoming aware that writing takes particular conventional forms in different contexts. How can both subject lecturers and writing specialists help students understand the issues related to academic writing, which include taking a stance, developing an argument, addressing a specific audience, and choosing the appropriate writing style? How can we help students in the often-difficult process of writing itself?

This chapter outlines many of the issues facing subject lecturers and writing specialists when considering how to help students improve their writing. We aim to:

- introduce text-based approaches to teaching general features of writing that characterise different text types, their structure and rhetorical purposes;
- consider the rhetorical purposes of text types, particularly the notion of 'argument' in relation to rhetorical purpose in academic writing,

and highlight the function of evidence and synthesis in building argument;

- look at aspects of writing that constitute register, including degrees of formality, the personal voice and linguistic accuracy;
- introduce process-based approaches to teaching writing, including the stages of prewriting, drafting and polishing a text; the use of peer review, and issues related to collaborative writing;
- discuss how to integrate the teaching of the writing process with teaching specific text types and disciplinary forms of writing.

THE PURPOSES OF WRITING

If you consider why you ask students to write, you may find a variety of reasons, including the following, discussed in Chapter 1: as assessment; as an aid to critical thinking, understanding and memory; to extend students' learning beyond lectures and other formal meetings; to improve students' communication skills; and to train students as future professionals in particular disciplines. This range of reasons for writing may not be so apparent to students, who may see writing as mainly an assessment hurdle. Below we outline an activity to help students explore these issues.

Activity 2.1 An introduction to the purposes of writing

1   Ask students to brainstorm individually all the types of writing they have done in the last few weeks (e.g. shopping lists, text messages, notes on lectures, experimental results, birthday cards, poetry).

2   In small groups have students put the different types of writing into some form of classification. You might want to suggest functional classifications such as *memory aids, social communication, learning about x, for assessment.* Some forms of writing will fall into more than one category.

3   In a whole-class discussion, narrow the focus to academic writing activities such as notes made on reading or in lectures, essay drafts, and laboratory reports. Discuss the purposes of the different types of academic writing students have done. Ask students to consider the different audiences for these types of writing, the specific rhetorical purpose of this form of writing, and the kinds of language, information, and evidence they will need to draw upon. Extend the discussion to include other types of writing students will do in the future.

In considering these purposes for academic writing and the usefulness of discussing them with students we take the position that certain *general* aspects of academic writing can be isolated and taught. In the next sections we outline the features of many types of academic writing that can usefully be made explicit to students; we then discuss different approaches to teaching the process of writing and finally look at ways of integrating a focus on the writing process with a concern for the final text.

TEACHING WRITING: FOCUS ON TEXT

In this section we look at some specific features of academic text including text types, rhetorical purpose, register and linguistic accuracy. While many of these features may seem obvious, often students, especially those just entering tertiary education, find it far from straightforward to know exactly what is expected.

Text types

Words such as 'essay', 'laboratory report' and 'case study' are problematic in that they denote a wide variety of types of text. For ease of reference in discussing text types we continue to use these labels, but we emphasise that you cannot assume that the knowledge of what to expect in a certain text type is shared by students. The essay, for example, may contain different elements depending on whether it is framed as a critical review, a discussion, a personal response or an exposition. Our implicit knowledge of what to expect from text types in response to certain prompts, such as 'discuss', 'critically evaluate', 'compare and contrast', informs the judgements that we make about the success of students' texts as a whole. The way we can generalise text types enables us as teachers to isolate certain traits and make them explicit to students, but we need to bear in mind that text types vary in response to the function that a text performs, which is not always reflected in the descriptive term applied to it.

Consider the types of writing that you ask your students to do. Would you classify them as essays, reports, reviews? Do you think your students are clear on what they are required to do in each of these text types?

Probably the most commonly labelled text type is the essay. Most students will have been taught a basic essay outline – introduction, body and conclusion – at school. This linear structure represents a particular preference of Anglo-American academic writing (Reid, 1984) that students from other cultures may need to be made aware of. The alternative title of 'argument essay' highlights one of the reasons for the pre-eminence of this text type in academic writing. It has evolved as a vehicle for synthesis, opinion, and theory, all of which may imply argument of different sorts and which help to account for the disparate nature of what is known as an essay. In Figure 2.1, we present two text types, an argument essay (in this case in the form of an *exposition*, that is, with arguments presented both for and against) and a project report, with their functional stages labelled on the left and a more explicit description on the right. If your students write texts using similar formats you may want to adapt these outlines to make clear for them what the

Figure 2.1 Two typical text types and their functional organisation

The argument essay outline

Functional stages	*Description*
(Introduction) Overall position/ argument	Here you usually indicate how you will approach the topic, and provide a statement of the main argument (thesis statement/point of view).
(Body) Sub-arguments and supporting evidence	Here you put forward sub-arguments with each one linking (explicitly or implicitly) to your overall position. Evidence to support main and sub-arguments is presented and evaluated. Further arguments and evidence may then be presented and evaluated. Counter-evidence may be presented and evaluated, usually negatively. This process continues until the case for your main argument is strong.
(Conclusion) Reinforcement of overall position/ argument	Here you provide an overall summary of the arguments and evidence together with a final evaluation. This reinforces the position you took in the introduction.
References	List the works you have mentioned in the text.

continued …

Figure 2.1 continued

The investigative project report outline[1]

Functional stages	Description
Aims	This stage is a full account of what you were trying to find out and why it was important. If a project proposal was written, then any subsequent changes should be noted and briefly explained.
Literature review	Here you discuss the ideas which are relevant to your project. This should show that you understand the background issues and theories relating to the project.
Methodology	This should be a description of the methods used and will include any alterations that became necessary during the conduct of the investigation. Your choice of method should be drawn from or build upon the literature review.
An account of your conduct of the investigation	Here you should describe the context in which the work was carried out and give a concise account of what was done. Explain how you addressed any critical issues. It may be written as a first-person narrative or more formally.
Findings	In this stage give the results of the investigation. How do these relate to issues in the literature? Present examples from the evidence collected to illustrate the points being made.
Evaluation	Here you need to consider the outcome of the project in relation to the initial aims and questions. Are there ways in which it could be changed and improved if carried out again? What kinds of further investigation could be made to follow up the results or extend the work started?
References	A list of all sources of material quoted or drawn upon in the project.
Appendices	Additional data or analysis that supports your aims and findings.

expectations of these text types are in your disciplinary area. You will find outlines of other text types in Chapter 3.

These broad outlines offer a first step in making writing expectations explicit. The conventions of particular text types and disciplines may be best demonstrated using example texts. Whole texts or sections of texts that exemplify good practice can be culled from the work of previous students and even made available on-line, as some university departments are doing (see Chapter 6).

Signposting text structure

While the writer of a text may have an overview of its basic text type structure, it is still necessary to alert the reader to its elements. Student writers often need to learn how to use aspects of *metadiscourse*, that is, language that refers to things happening in the text itself (Brandt, 1990) to 'signpost' their movements through the structure of their writing. At the later stages of writing students can add signposts such as transitional words or phrases that help guide the reader from one section to another; sentences that recap the main idea of the preceding section, or words that signal agreement, extension, qualification, or objections to previously stated ideas. You may find it useful to discuss or provide students with the list in Figure 2.2 on the different kinds of meaning relations signalled by different conjunctions. You could ask students to identify several conjunctions they have used in a recent piece of writing and to check, using Figure 2.2, whether they think they have chosen the most appropriate one. You might also encourage students to add to the list.

Rhetorical purpose

In Chapter 1 we discussed rhetorical purpose in terms of the overt communicative purpose of a text. Text types such as laboratory reports have

Figure 2.2 Signposting conjunctions

Conjunctions to express different kinds of meaning relations

Temporal: when, while, after, before, then
Causative: because, if, although, so that, therefore
Adversative: however, alternatively, although, nevertheless, while
Additive: and, or, similarly, incidentally

(Love, 1999: 202)

---

as their overt purpose to report on experiments, while case studies text types report and make recommendations. However, there are also implicit purposes which may not be clear to students and to illustrate what we mean we look here at the use of the term 'argument'. In some instances lecturers use 'argument' almost synonymously with the organisational structure of the text type – which section should come first, second, etc. It is also used to emphasise the linking of ideas at a 'local' or sentence and paragraph level, as this marker's comment indicates: 'Too many unlinked facts here. I can't see any argument' (Lea and Street, 1998: 166). The notion of argument is also used when lecturers demand that students provide greater referencing to source material both to 'prove' a particular point (e.g. 'Where is your evidence?') and to demonstrate understanding. Argument may also mean a perspective, a position or stance on something. The list in Activity 2.2 includes a variety of conceptions of what is meant by argument.

It may be your conception of argument is different. However you use the term, it is important to explain what you mean to student writers, not least because the model of argument that many student writers bring with them from school is a 'for and against' debating model in which points for and against a particular position are listed, with a brief conclusion outlining the student's perspective. Activity 2.2 is a way of asking students to consider what is implied by argument in academic writing. The activity equates argument with taking a stance or position on what is being written about. It identifies some of the ways in which the concept of arguing in academic writing is presented.

The advantage of using an abstract such as this is that it contains many of the elements students need to identify in a short piece of text. For example, in responding to the question, students should note that Shields gives us his view of a nineteenth-century model in the first sentence then asserts that it is not applicable today in sentences two and three. He offers a new approach in sentence four. He thus argues that his new approach deals better with contemporary realities than an old approach. His argument rests on an acceptance that the old model is flawed and that his new approach overcomes its shortcomings. This is a version of the common technique of reviewing past literature and finding weaknesses or areas for development, then proposing new ideas to deal with them. You could follow up this analysis by asking students to write a similar abstract or assignment which outlines the stance that they are taking.

Activity 2.2 Argument and academic writing

Students are commonly told to:

- take up a position
- adopt a particular perspective
- put forward points for and against a particular position
- explore possible positions
- link theory and evidence
- draw a conclusion
- analyse
- be critical
- develop a central idea
- use evidence to support an argument
- express personal opinions
- use personal interpretation.[2]

1   In groups or pairs ask students to discuss one or two of these expressions in relation to a recent or forthcoming piece of writing. Do they see their own writing as putting forward an argument or stating facts? How can they evaluate the status of the 'facts' they are writing about?

2   With more advanced students, use an abstract such as that below, or an actual assignment from your discipline to identify the argument being put forward and the textual strategies used.

A division of social processes into different, mutually exclusive 'value spheres' such as 'cultural' or 'economic' derives from a nineteenth-century, European model of civil society. This model cannot respond to current political demands for cultural recognition and redistributive justice which characterise multi-cultural societies. It does not acknowledge the economic importance of knowledge work. Spatially located analyses, such as in urban and regional research, offer an ideal opportunity to marry analytical approaches to capture the convergences of cultural and economic processes in given localities. Attempts within political economy to integrate culture as a force of governance have tended to oversimplify the cultural aspects of economic activity as, for example, discourse. A 'cultural-economic' approach emphasising place and context is proposed.

(Shields, 1999: 303)

This activity highlights the often covert function of academic texts; that is, to persuade readers to your point of view through a well-constructed argument which lays out logical reasoning and evidence. It is often not obvious that a research report in science is a text designed to convince the reader that the experimental method and results are valid, in the same way that an essay in literature may be designed to persuade the reader to a new view of a fictional character's motivation.

Much of the persuasive purpose of academic argument is accomplished through synthesising past research and presenting evidence to back up claims or points of view. However, students may not understand this particularly if in school they used textbooks or notes prepared by teachers. Understanding that academic writers often summarise and synthesise the work of others will help students overcome the idea that citing sources is tantamount to admitting that the work is not their own. Students may then appreciate the dual importance of referencing their sources: a) to give credit where it is due to the work of others; and b) to enable readers themselves to find these sources.

What counts as suitable evidence to support an argument is governed by the *epistemic conventions* of a discipline. Epistemic conventions refer to the means of establishing 'truth' as based on accepted forms of evidence. The nature of the evidence may be qualitative, quantitative or both. It can include empirical research done by the student or drawn from readings, statistical data, examples or illustrations. Again, students should be aware of the existence of cultural preferences for sources of evidence. For example, Western academic writing does not usually accept religious scriptures or personal anecdotes as compelling evidence. You can help students support their arguments by discussing the types of evidence valued in their particular field and how to present it. They also need to understand how to evaluate their sources of evidence. In the field of history, for instance, if students are using primary sources (that is, documents from the historical period), they need to consider the reliability of such documents, as, for example, with the personal nature of any observations. In the sciences, it is particularly significant to know how up-to-date sources are. Thus, to stress the importance of new research, one biology lecturer insists that students include references to at least three recent journal articles in their essays.

This section has introduced the problematic nature of specifying rhetorical purpose, particularly with reference to the lack of explicitness over terms such as argument. As argument is such a central concept in academic writing, we will return to it throughout the book. We next move to consider how to help students understand the characteristics of academic register.

Register

Register, as mentioned in Chapter 1, includes a range of linguistic aspects that are related to the contexts in which authors write. Among others, these include formality, sentence structure, specialist terminology, and the personal voice. By *formality* we mean the use of technical, elevated or abstract vocabulary, complex sentence structures and the avoidance of the personal voice (*I, you*). If we think of formality as a cline from the most formal (e.g. the language of legal documents) to the most informal (e.g. electronic mail between friends), most academic writing falls nearer to the legal documents than the friendly email.

Register is perhaps most easily explained to students by discussing some of the differences between informal speech and formal writing, for example, a conversation between friends compared with a job application letter. In spoken language the grammar or the ways in which ideas are linked together is complex or intricate. In writing, in contrast, many ideas get packed into fewer words, primarily through a greater variety of *lexical items*, or vocabulary. It may be useful to explicitly compare spoken with written language as part of your teaching or in making comments as feedback on students' writing. You could use Activity 2.3 with students to raise the issue of academic register.

In answering question 4 you could discuss typical features of the academic register such as:

- *High lexical density*: Large number of vocabulary items other than verbs per clause (e.g. 'A significant commitment of time must be made in the production of a lengthy work').
- *Highly nominal style*: Greater use of nouns than verbs (underlined below) to construct meanings and make them compact (e.g. 'The production of a manuscript necessarily <u>involves</u> issues of time management', rather than 'To <u>produce</u> a manuscript you <u>need to consider</u> how to <u>manage</u> time efficiently').
- *Impersonal constructions*: Subjects or agents of clauses often back-grounded (e.g. 'It is often difficult to incorporate an additional workload into an already heavy agenda', rather than 'You may find it difficult to …').
- *Hedging and emphasising*: Verbs and phrases used to modify statements made (e.g. *may, might, must, need to, it seems that, possibly, probably*).

Activity 2.3 Formality in writing

The following two extracts both introduce the problem of how to plan a schedule when working on a manuscript. There are, however, major variations in register between them. Your task is to analyse the selections by answering the following questions.

1   Who is a likely audience for each selection?
2   Why would one selection be preferable over another?
3   What argument would the author give for choosing one over another?
4   What aspects of language are involved in achieving the different registers?

A. Looking ahead and planning your schedule

So, you have a manuscript in your life? As demanding as a jealous lover and as burdensome as unpaid debts, the weight of this new presence can be difficult to cope with when you may already be juggling family, a job, studies, friends, and perhaps a hobby or exercise programme. A little planning can make the load easier to bear ...

B. Time management and manuscript production

The production of a manuscript necessarily involves issues of time management. A significant commitment of time must be made in the production of a lengthy work therefore several factors should be considered from the onset. It is often difficult to incorporate an additional workload into an already heavy agenda, and so, time management planning is essential to successful completion of the project ...

(Zuengler, 1999)

How far these features of register are characteristic of the writing you expect from students will depend partly on your discipline specialism; register is by definition dependent on the context in which writing takes place. Hyland (2000), for example, noted at one extreme an average of 0.7 occurrences of personal pronouns per 1,000 words in textbooks in biology, in contrast to 5.7 occurrences per 1,000 words in philosophy. For much of the twentieth century, particularly in the sciences, the notion of objectivity meant that there was no place for a personal voice. This tradition continued into advice for student writers, particularly in scientific fields, until quite recently:

Scientific writing is not of a personal or conversational nature and for this reason the third person is commonly used. As a general rule, personal pronouns such as *I, we, you, me, my, our* and *us* should not appear except in quotations.

(Anderson and Poole, 1994: 6)

Activity 2.4 The use of personal voice in academic writing

1   Read students the quotation from Anderson and Poole above and ask them to consider whether they think this advice holds true for their disciplinary area.

2   Provide examples from your own discipline and ask students to note references to the writer. In some disciplines and in some types of writing, there is often a shift back and forth between a depersonalised style (*It is argued that ... Readings were taken at five-minute intervals ...*) and greater writer visibility (*I have argued that ... I consider that future work in this area ...*).

3   Using the same disciplinary texts as in 2, ask students to look specifically at ways that writing is depersonalised, for example, with the use of passive voice (*The participants were given questionnaires ...*), the use of *one* or *it* as subject (*One might question whether ...*), the placing of processes instead of active participants at the beginning of the sentence (*Observation of the rats over a three month period allowed ...*). Discuss what happens in the text with such depersonalisation in terms of, for example, how the passive can obscure who is taking responsibility for the actions described in the text, and what kind of emphasis the use of these techniques gives to aspects of the text. Ask students to consider the effects of using such strategies in their own writing.

In the interests of making science writing clearer and more accessible, references to *I* and *we* are increasing, though how acceptable they are to you as the reader and marker of your students' work needs to be made explicit. Activity 2.4 provides ways which can be used separately or together to explore with your students the conventions within your discipline that relate to using a personal voice.

Linguistic accuracy

Complaints about students' spelling and grammar often figure in press reports, with headlines such as 'It's official: grammar's gone downhill, and 'Oxford undergraduates can't spell' (*The Times Higher Education Supplement*, 13 February 1998, quoted in Crème and Lea, 1999). Whether or not such reports are justified, errors in spelling and grammar certainly

Figure 2.3 Patterns of spelling error

Substitution e.g. s for c, y for i (*absense, arbitraryness*)
Omission e.g. single consonant for double, omission of vowel, consonant or syllable (*accomodate, unhinderd, condem, expement*)
Reversals, delays, anticipation e.g. reversal of vowels or consonants; delays or anticipation of consonants (*recieve, perscriptive, regconise*)
Homophones i.e. using words that sound the same but are spelt differently (your/you're, their/they're/there, hear/here, illicit/elicit, principle/principal; practice/practise, two/to/too)
Other e.g. likely typographical error or slip, archaism

(Based on Wray, 1996: 99–100)

---

generate strong feelings, with lecturers often becoming frustrated at what they feel are 'basic' errors. If spelling and grammar are areas in students' writing that you want to respond to, it is important to do so in ways which will help students to improve. For instance, if you notice that certain words are commonly misspelt by your students, you could compile a list of the relevant correct spellings and distribute it before students do their written work.

You may find the classification of spelling errors in students' essays in Figure 2.3 useful when identifying and making comments on students' spelling. Students could be introduced to the main category headings in the table and encouraged to record their patterns of errors with your help.

Spelling and grammar errors combine in the case of the apostrophe in English. Much confusion is caused because the usage of 's in everyday contexts (such as shop signs) is changing. Students may not be familiar with the rules governing the use of specific elements, for example where the 's/s/s' should be used. It would be useful to provide students with patterns of standard usage, as in Figure 2.4.

If you are concerned about spelling in students' writing, consider directing them to specific resources such as spelling dictionaries and other reference works such as *Collins Cobuild Guide 6: Homophones* and Payne (1995) on *Spelling*. Most importantly, if spelling is part of your assessment criteria, you need to make sure that students know this.

So far we have concentrated mainly on spelling accuracy, but errors of grammar are also something that you may want to help students with. In the same way that we advocated drawing students' attention to

Figure 2.4 The apostrophe

The apostrophe 's': when to put 's and when not to The basic rules of use are as follows:

1   Put an apostrophe before the 's' to indicate singular possession (except with 'its') and after the 's' to indicate plural possession, for example: *The student's* (one student) *essay was very good*; *The students'* (more than one student) *essays were very good.*

2   There is no apostrophe in a plural, for example: *Philosophers have studied* ... ; *Different conclusions have been reached...* .

3   Put an apostrophe before the 's' in abbreviations of the verb forms is/has, for example: *It's (it is) a well established fact that* ...; *She's (she has) had many books published on this area...* . The ' indicates that something has been removed.

---

common errors and correct spelling patterns, you could use Figure 2.5 to alert students to the problems you as a marker often observe.

Students whose first language is not English often have significant difficulties with some aspects of English grammar that are distinct from the problems that native English speakers have. These include: choice of article, *a, an* or *the*; word order; prepositions, *on, at, in*, etc. Often universities provide English language support for them and you may be able to arrange 'team teaching' if you have large numbers of international students. Team teaching is when language specialists, for example, record lectures and then work with the subject specialist to design materials to support students in their learning of both the language and the content. It is beyond the scope of this book to examine the writing problems of international students in detail. However, in addition to seeking help within your institution there are many texts at various levels useful to students.[3]

In dealing with text types, rhetorical purpose, register and grammatical accuracy we have focused on features of the final written text. We turn now to ways of helping students with the process of producing that writing.

TEACHING WRITING: FOCUS ON PROCESS

In the history of writing instruction, as Chapter 1 discussed, researchers and teachers have oscillated between focusing on the written product

Figure 2.5 Some common grammatical errors in student writing

---

1   Not putting a main verb in each sentence
    Example: Considering all positions.
    Alternative: All positions are being considered. *Or*: Having considered all positions, the most convincing is that advanced by Thomas (1983).

2   Lack of pronoun agreement in sentences
    Example: The teacher has a responsibility towards their students.
    Alternative: The teacher has a responsibility towards her/his students.

3   Unclear use of indefinite reference words – pronouns such as *it, they, that, those*
    Example: This is an important area to consider. (Unclear what 'this' refers to.)

4   Inconsistent use of tenses/modes
    Example: Pupils must have confidence in their ability before they could actually succeed in examinations.
    Alternative: Pupils must have confidence in their ability before they can actually succeed in examinations.

5   Influence of speech on writing
    Example: He could of examined the situation more carefully.
    Alternative: He could have examined the situation more carefully.

                                                          (Based on Lillis, 1996: 97)

---

that students are meant to produce, and focusing on the creative processes of writing, the role of the individual in the act of writing, and the social aspects of writing, including students' identities, disciplinary conventions, and the larger social context (Galbraith and Rijlaarsdam, 1999). Our view is that all these aspects need to be taken into account in teaching writing. In this section we look at the processes involved in academic writing, including process approaches, collaborative writing, and using peer review (see Elbow, 1981).

Whether students write in response to a set assignment or are asked to develop their own topics, many students are daunted by the act of writing itself. Process approaches focus primarily on what writers do as they write rather than on textual features, but depending on the writer's immediate task, these approaches may also consider text features. As Figure 2.6 shows, the process approach includes different stages, which can be combined with other aspects of teaching writing, for example,

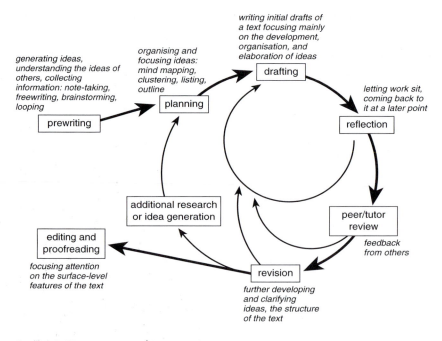

Figure 2.6 The writing process approach

the study of textual features. Not all writers move through the stages included in process approaches; some stages may be helpful and others superfluous to any given writing task. However, many students carry the notion that the writings of published authors have sprung fully formed from their heads.

Process approaches are premised on the notion that writing is an iterative process, as shown in Figure 2.6, involving the techniques described below (Murray, 1987). Stages of the writing process can happen in various orders at different points. Lecturers can help clarify students' misconceptions about writing by explicitly teaching the stages of the writing process as described in Figure 2.6 (Curry, 1996).

Prewriting techniques

Prewriting strategies such as brainstorming and freewriting (explained below) can help writers find ideas, collect information, activate tacit knowledge, and organise their thoughts. In describing these strategies here we do not mean to downplay the important work of discovery that often occurs while drafting. However, although experienced writers may identify, invent, and refine their ideas while they are writing, students often find it helpful to think about ideas before trying to create a formal text. Some of these strategies can be used well by the writer alone; others work better in pairs or in small groups.

In *brainstorming* students spark ideas off each other after a discussion or reading. Ideally, students throw ideas into a non-judgemental forum, with the goal of generating multiple ideas on a topic without immediately evaluating their suitability for development. The lecturer or a student lists the ideas generated by the group on the blackboard to create a record. An individual writer can also brainstorm about a topic, although input from others will be missing. Figure 2.7 illustrates a brainstorm for a social sciences essay.

In *freewriting* an author writes literally without ceasing within a set time limit of, for example, ten minutes, starting with a particular topic related to the subject under study (for instance, immigration in Figure 2.7). Freewriting is messy, unplanned, and unpredictable but students find it useful for activating often-tacit knowledge on a topic, identifying

Figure 2.7 Brainstorm on 'issues related to immigration'

Brainstorm: issues related to immigration

Add to labour force
Skills shortages in industrialised countries, e.g. teachers
Low-level jobs – agriculture, cleaning, service work, etc.
High-skill work – information technology, other occupations
Declining populations of industrialised countries
Need to support ageing populations
Immigrants pay taxes on earnings and investments
Entrepreneurs bringing energy, new skills
Higher fertility rate among many groups of immigrants
Benefits of multiculturalism: arts, religion, food
Greater demands on educational system
Bring new ideas to workplace; new views on old problems
Bi/multilingual education
Cultural issues in education, e.g. Muslim girls wearing headscarves
Discrimination/racism against immigrants
Don't share local prejudices
Fears of native population about job loss
Issues of learning language, new culture
Hard working, need to 'make it'

---

paths for exploration, and for quieting the 'editor' that scrutinises every word we write. Lecturers can even take some lecture time for a brief session of freewriting on a topic related to course material as a way to warm students up to writing and thinking. Usually lecturers do not evaluate or even collect freewriting. With practice (and enforced discipline from the lecturer), students learn that freewriting can be a low-pressure strategy for writing without worrying about the quality of the output. Freewriting reinforces the principle that it is possible to separate the idea-generating phases of writing from more critical editorial stages.

Journal writing

Alongside brainstorming and freewriting the keeping of journals can also constitute another form of prewriting. Student journals can serve multiple functions and take various forms, from bound notebooks to electronic mail entries. Journals provide an opportunity for an informal, personal type of writing in which students can make observations, reflect on questions set by the lecturer, respond to course materials, and ask questions without the constraints of creating a formal text. In this case journals can be used as vehicles for student learning and include both their preliminary responses to set assignments or questions as well as students' own explorations. Students can draw on the ideas they develop in journal entries as they craft their more formal, assessed texts. Many students, including non-native English speakers, benefit from the frequent practice that writing regular journal entries can provide.

Although it is time consuming, when lecturers can review and respond to students' journals it may be a rare opportunity to engage in one-to-one dialogue. Some lecturers collect and respond to students' journals once or twice a term; others with smaller groups may review journals on a weekly basis. Ideally lecturers' responses will attend to the content of the journals and not to errors in linguistic accuracy. Such responses can stimulate students' thinking and help them focus their ideas for writing. Lecturers can promote dialogue by requiring students to respond in subsequent journal entries to the comments and questions that lecturers make. Chapter 4 discusses the assessment of journals and reflective writing that asks students to consider their learning process as a formal part of a course, often in applied areas such as health and medicine. In these cases, the rhetorical purpose of journal writing expands to include reflection for assessment purposes as well as personal academic development.

From generative techniques such as brainstorming, freewriting and journals, the next stage is for the writer to begin to organise and order ideas. The terms *mind mapping*, *clustering*, and *branching* describe graphic organising techniques. Many writers find it helpful to see a visual representation of ideas at the early stages of organising. As an example, Figure 2.8 takes the brainstorm on immigration from Figure 2.7 and begins to organise the ideas by mapping them out. Students can review the ideas resulting from prewriting for those that fit together, those that may be extraneous to the task, and those that need further investigation or development.

Some writers move from graphic representations to use more formal organisational techniques such as writing a *list* or an *essay plan* (outline). These plans or outlines may be drawn up to match the expectations set by certain text types, such as an argument essay in social science, for example. For inexperienced writers such plans can help identify gaps in the development of ideas, arguments, and sources of evidence. Plans can be written according to the pattern that combines Arabic numerals, upper case letters, and Roman numerals, lower case letters (e.g. 1, A, ii, a) or by using the 'scientific' pattern of Arabic numerals and full stops (e.g. 1.1, 1.2). Outlines can be especially helpful in organising one's thoughts for an extended piece of writing; when drafting (see below) begins, some writers prefer to start in the middle of a plan rather than with the introduction to the text. Figure 2.9 develops an outline for a social sciences expositional essay from the cluster diagram in Figure 2.8. Note the shift from clustering ideas to building an argument.[4]

Drafting

As noted, a fundamental principle of process approaches is that writing is an iterative process. Thus, where possible, writing assignments or tasks should build from opportunities for students to revise a piece of work in response to feedback from peer reviewers (see below) or the lecturer (see Chapter 5).

Indeed, one-off, assessed tasks tend to limit possibilities for growth in the writer's ideas and modes of expression. Students are more likely to attend to feedback from lecturers about their writing if they will have an

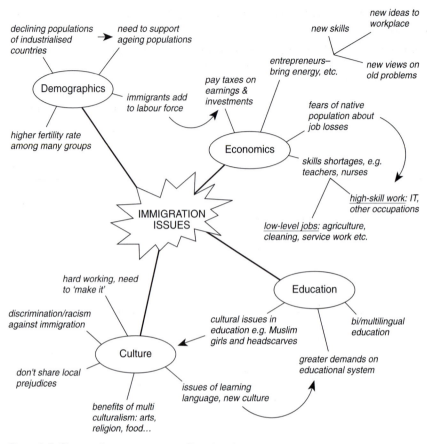

Figure 2.8 Cluster diagram on issues of immigration

opportunity to re-work it. Furthermore, students who write and re-draft their work have less opportunity to present plagiarised work as their own, since the lecturer may have seen earlier versions of it (see Chapter 4 for more on plagiarism). Of course students who must write tests in an examination have only one opportunity to write. But when writing essays, reports, or other texts outside an exam, students often benefit from the opportunity to revisit and resubmit pieces of work.

In an initial draft, the writer's focus should be on developing meaning, using ideas gathered in prewriting strategies. Topic development may involve narrowing down a broad focus, or removing or adding information where appropriate. At this stage writers, including non-native speakers of English, should try to avoid being overly concerned with linguistic accuracy unless it interferes with making meaning. Once students have completed a first or second draft on their own, the next

Figure 2.9 Outline on the economic benefits of immigration

Outline: 'The Benefits of Immigration to Industrialised Countries'
Position/argument: immigrants provide net economic and cultural benefits to industrialised countries.

I   Background: industrialised countries
    A.   Demographic changes
        1.   ageing population
           (a)   (evidence)
           (b)   (evidence)
        2.   zero or negative population growth
           (a)   (evidence)
    B.   Changes in labour force
        1.   reduced work force, especially in low-level service and agricultural jobs
        2.   ageing work force may lack contemporary skills
        3.   new ideas needed for old problems

II   Benefits of immigration
    A.   Demographics
        1.   higher birth rate among many immigrant groups
        2.   younger average age of immigrants
    B.   Labour features
        1.   hard workers willing to do many jobs native-born population eschews (e.g. agricultural and service work)
        2.   entrepreneurs with particular skills, knowledge and drive
        3.   pay more in taxes than receive in social services

III Cultural issues
    A.   Benefits of multiculturalism
        1.   bring diversity in an increasingly global world
        2.   retain connections with people in other countries
    B.   Difficulties related to immigration
        1.   immigrants may face discrimination and racism
        2.   immigrants face issues of adaptation/acculturation (e.g. Muslim schoolgirls who want to wear headscarves)
        3.   immigrants may need to learn a new language
        4.   require greater government provision of bi/multilingual education

IV   Conclusion
    A.   Challenges for both immigrants and the industrialised countries
        1.   challenges for immigrants: language, work, education, culture, etc.
        2.   challenges for countries: education, discrimination, etc.
    B.   Advantages of immigration outweigh the disadvantages
        1.   some disadvantages
        2.   economic advantages
        3.   cultural advantages

stage calls for review by peers or the lecturer.[5] Structured opportunities for revision help develop students as writers, as ideally they internalise the sorts of responses that readers make to their work.

Peer review

A key aspect of writing process approaches is the importance of seeking and responding to the feedback of others while a text is under development. Feedback on students' drafts may take the form of oral or written comments by peers or the lecturer designed to guide students in their revisions (Chapter 5 focuses on providing such feedback). Students may feel that lecturers' feedback is most important because of lecturers' expert knowledge of the topic. They also may not feel competent to provide useful advice to each other. However, relying entirely on lecturer feedback can bring certain disadvantages for students' intellectual development. Because of lecturers' power to mark assignments, students may feel compelled to incorporate lecturers' suggestions (or directives) in subsequent revisions even if they disagree or do not understand them. With training and practice, students can fruitfully engage in peer review, which can help them develop their critical faculties and understand how other readers respond to their writing. For advanced or postgraduate students, engaging in peer review can function as a rehearsal for the peer review that occurs in professional academic settings. In order for peer review to be successful, lecturers need to explain and ideally model it, whether students engage in peer review during lecture time or on their own (Berg, 2000).

Peer review can occur within pairs or small groups that may be set up to do one assignment or to work together over an extended period. These groups or pairs could also work together throughout the prewriting and organising stages of writing to help each other develop plans for writing. In any case, students should provide each other with copies of the text for peers to review in advance (such drafts may be circulated electronically via electronic mail or conferencing, as Chapter 6 notes). If peer review occurs during lectures, a fair amount of time should be allotted for the process, as it is time-consuming. One option is to go through the process once during a lecture and subsequently for students to meet informally for peer review sessions. The guidelines in Activity 2.5 can support students in effective peer review.

Activity 2.5 Student guidelines for peer review

1   Before the meeting: in a covering note or email to members of the review group, the author should explain the purpose of the text and how it relates to the assignment (e.g. if a choice has been possible among various questions). If the lecturer has distributed assignment criteria reviewers should use these as well in responding to the draft. Next the author should focus the peer reviewers on areas of the text that have been difficult to write. While reading the text, peer reviewers should make written comments on a copy of it that they will later give to the author.

2   In the peer group meeting, the author listens and takes notes while the reviewers respond to the content, structure, argument, use of evidence, etc. Reviewers should not pay much attention to errors of linguistic accuracy unless they interfere with understanding the meaning of the text.

3   After peer reviewers respond, the author may ask clarifying questions or try to reconcile conflicting comments or suggestions with the help of the group. Finally, the author should try to summarise a strategy for responding to the reviewers' comments in subsequent revisions.

Chapter 4 discusses some assessment issues related to group work, including how to assess individual contributions to a collective endeavour. However, one way to assess whether the process (apart from the final product) of peer review is working well is by students submitting their various drafts of a text along with the written comments of the peer reviewers. Students may not have revised their texts in accordance with the suggestions of peer reviewers, but there should be some evidence that they have considered reasonable suggestions.

Reflection

In the iterative cycle of process approaches delineated in Figure 2.6, *reflection* means letting a piece of writing sit before coming back to it with a fresh pair of eyes, and perhaps with feedback from peers or the lecturer. Even without input from others, reflection time can allow writers to see gaps in their text structure, use of evidence, etc., and to note infelicitous phrasings.

Editing and proofreading

Finally, an author must let go of a text and make it public. The final stages of writing consist of editing, proofreading, and polishing a text.

Here students should attend to the mechanics of writing, including formatting, references and footnotes, and issues of linguistic accuracy. Again students can work in pairs to review each other's work. Students may be encouraged to use computer spelling check programmes but not to limit their review of errors to those noted by the computer. All students may benefit from the information and examples of usage given in dictionaries and reference books written for non-native English speakers (e.g. *Collins Cobuild English Dictionary, Longman Dictionary of Contemporary English, Oxford Advanced Learner's Dictionary*). Chapter 4 provides a student checklist for self-assessment that you may wish to modify for your context and students, and supply as part of the drafting and editing/proofreading stages.

Collaborative writing

Our discussion above of the benefits of peer review to student writing assumed that each student writer would be responsible for 'authoring' the text, and that any assessment and marking would consider the work to be entirely by one student. Increasingly students are being asked to engage in collaborative writing, especially as part of projects in courses in applied disciplines such as business studies. In such cases, writing process approaches may be adapted to incorporate the contributions of a pair or group of students. In many ways process approaches work best in collaborative settings, that is, prewriting strategies such as brain-storming are highly effective in groups, and feedback on student writing may come as the result of peer review alone. When it comes to drafting texts collaboratively, students may be responsible for drafting different sections of the text and then combining them as versions of the text proceed. Chapter 4 discusses issues related to the assessment of collaborative writing. Chapter 6 notes that collaborative writing may be best achieved using technologies such as electronic mail and conferencing programmes.

In concluding this section we should reiterate that not all stages will be necessary for all students or in all contexts and that some of the stages can occur simultaneously. Students may need help in learning about these stages and practising them, but after such scaffolding, students may internalise them and no longer need you to formally review the stages.

In this section we have focused on ways of helping students with the process of writing in contrast to the text focus of the previous section.

However, we consider that they should not be seen as alternative approaches. You can mesh process with the textual and disciplinary concerns of subject lecturers. You can scaffold students learning to write in your academic disciplines by demonstrating the stages of the writing process that specifically relate to their context; that is, by using the stages to assist towards writing the text types that they will need most frequently. Students can then frame their drafts within the textual conventions of, for example, a case study in a business course, rather than a traditional essay. Students may still go through the initial stages of the writing process (prewriting and planning), but when they arrive at drafting, they would consider the conventions of the appropriate text type. The subsequent stages of the writing process could then continue. You may wish to introduce these notions in relation to a particular assignment you set within a course. Some of the stages will prove useful to students in preparation for traditional assignments including essay examinations; for others, such as re-drafting texts, to be most effective you may wish to reconsider how you set writing assignments.

INTEGRATING THE PROCESS APPROACH WITH TEXT ANALYSIS

In this final section we focus on one approach to integrating text and process in helping students write. In the *Teaching and learning cycle*,[6] lecturer and students work through phases which can be repeated as necessary. In the first phase – *Building the context* – activities to raise students' awareness of a topic and knowledge about it precede writing and can be linked to the prewriting techniques discussed above. The second phase – *Modelling and deconstruction* – is an opportunity for students to examine example target texts and identify specific aspects such as text type and register. *Joint construction* – the third phase – is a form of collaborative writing with the lecturer playing a key role in scaffolding students' writing by guiding the joint construction of a text type (on an overhead transparency or projected computer screen). The fourth phase – *Independent construction* – is where the scaffolding of the earlier phases is withdrawn and students write final texts on their own or within groups, frequently participating in a form of peer review. These stages simultaneously integrate developing awareness of text and process to help students see how particular uses of language contribute to building an effective piece of discipline-specific writing. Once internalised, students can use strategies learnt through the process approach or the teaching and learning cycle to analyse academic texts, or to review their writing approaches. In this way they are helped to envision the shape and structure of their texts and the linguistic choices they make in their writing and thereby become more accomplished and autonomous writers.

CONCLUSION

This chapter started with some of the issues related to teaching student writing that university lecturers might face, as in the case of Iain, the psychology lecturer. We have presented easily generalised aspects of teaching writing which can be adapted for use by subject specialist lecturers with or without the help of writing support tutors. Attention to features such as text type, rhetorical structure, register, and linguistic accuracy preceded a discussion of ways in which to encourage the writing process. Adapting the ideas to suit your students and the time you have available should ultimately result in students requiring less intervention from you on writing matters. Chapter 3 moves on from this 'general' focus on writing to examine in more detail the conventions and requirements of writing within particular academic disciplines.

NOTES

1 Based on the Open University publication: *E300 Assignment Book and Project Guide*, 2002b: 15.
2 This list is an adapted and expanded version of Crème and Lea, 1997: 34.
3 For general help with grammar at an advanced level they could consult, for example, Hewings, 1999a or Swan, 1995. More specific work on academic writing is provided by Swales and Feak, 1994 and 2000.
4 For space reasons we have not specified the evidence to support the argument, which would come at the next level down in the outline.
5 With large writing projects it can also be fruitful for lecturers to review students' detailed outlines or essay plans even before they begin to draft their texts, in order to focus on the development of ideas and arguments.
6 Rothery, 1996 gives a detailed explanation in the context of school education; Feez, 2001 discusses the teaching and learning cycle within the context of migrant education in Australia.

Chapter 3

Writing for different disciplines

Conflicting advice to students across disciplines[1]

Paul

This is a very promising start to your study of modern political history. You have argued your case well and supported it with appropriate documentary evidence...

Paul

You really have a problem with this essay, mainly for the reason that it is incoherent. It has no beginning, middle and end, no structure, no argument. May I suggest very strongly that you go to the Study Centre and make more enquiries about essay writing clinics...

INTRODUCTION

These comments made by lecturers on Paul's writing (not his real name) give us an insight into the problems faced by students working across different disciplinary traditions. Paul's main subject is history which he successfully studied at A level. He has received positive feedback on essays written in both history and politics, but his anthropology lecturer perceives his essay writing technique to be a problem. Through analysing what the student had written Lea and Street (1998) conclude that it is knowledge of how to argue and how to support his arguments with evidence *in anthropology* that is the issue for Paul, not general essay writing technique. Increasing numbers of inter- and multi-disciplinary courses mean that more students are struggling to get to grips with the writing expectations in several different areas.

In this chapter we consider some of the different strategies that you can use to help students recognise and produce the kinds of writing that are valued in different disciplinary areas. In Chapter 2 we outlined a range of techniques for helping students to improve their academic writing in a general sense. Here we propose that students have greater control over their writing if they are helped by lecturers to develop an explicit awareness of how different disciplines employ different text types and how these text types construct and represent knowledge (both through their text structure and through their use of register).

Such an approach assumes that lecturers have an understanding of the role played by language in their discipline and that they have the time to develop this understanding in their students. Whilst recognising that this may be more easily achieved in partnership with writing or study skills experts, this chapter aims to help both lecturers and writing tutors identify important features of writing in particular disciplines. It also provides some practical teaching strategies. These are designed to provide scaffolding and guidance as students build their knowledge and understanding of a discipline and develop control of disciplinary forms of writing.

It is, of course, beyond the scope of this chapter to provide a detailed description of how language varies across each discipline and sub-discipline. Rather, we aim to provide an understanding of key linguistic differences and the most important types of writing that occur across four main discipline areas (see Figure 3.1). This highlights for all lecturers the varied roles that language plays both in their own general area of expertise and in the range of sub-disciplines that their students increasingly have to 'write their way into'.

Figure 3.1 A categorisation of disciplines and their typical written texts

Sciences	Social Sciences	Humanities/Arts	Applied Disciplines
Examples include:			
physics, chemistry, biology, geology	sociology, geography, economics, politics, cultural and media studies, psychology	English, history, languages, classics, fine art, religious studies, nursing	business and management, philosophy, music, engineering, health and social welfare
Typical text types:[2]			
Laboratory reports, project proposals and reports, fieldwork notes, essays, dissertations	*essays, project reports,* fieldwork notes, dissertations	*essays,* critical analysis, translations, projects	*essays, case studies,* dissertations, projects

Figure 3.1 shows a broad disciplinary categorisation and the typical types of writing carried out by students. We use this categorisation as a convenient way of grouping disciplines with certain similar characteristics, while acknowledging the complexity of demarcating disciplines and their affiliations. (For a more extensive discussion of the difficulties of making such categorisations and the fluidity within disciplinary areas see Becher and Trowler, 2001.) The overlap between methods and epistemologies in the various disciplines means that even within named disciplinary communities members often ally themselves with different overarching groups. Geography, for instance, which we have placed in the category of social science, could arguably have been categorised as a science or a humanities subject.

We use the disciplinary categorisation to focus on typical types of writing such as project proposals, essays and case studies. We highlight areas of similarity and difference between disciplines in terms of how they interpret different text types. For example, there is much overlap in the use of 'essay'. We also examine how different registers are used to construct disciplinary identity.

We discuss in particular:

- academic knowledge as a continuum from the sciences to the humanities
- writing up project proposals and laboratory reports using examples from the sciences
- representing quantitative and pictorial illustrative material and discipline-specific terminology with particular reference to the social sciences
- the characteristics of the argument essay with an illustration from the humanities
- the characteristics of the case study illustrated by examples from applied disciplinary fields.

SCIENCES TO THE HUMANITIES: ACADEMIC KNOWLEDGE AS A CONTINUUM

In discussing disciplinary writing we start with the most obvious contrast – the so-called 'harder' sciences and the 'softer' humanities. MacDonald (1994) discusses them in terms of a continuum (Figure 3.2). The sciences, at one end, are empirically based – new knowledge is accepted on the

SCIENCES	SOCIAL SCIENCES	HUMANITIES

←——————————————————————————→

Figure 3.2 The academic knowledge continuum

basis of often quantifiable experimental proof. The writing of science tends to reinforce this view with research articles foregrounding a gap in knowledge, a hypothesis related to this gap, and quantifiable experimentation and findings (Swales, 1981). Humanities subjects, on the other hand, are generally not quantitative in their methods. Knowledge about a subject is accepted or rejected on the basis of how well argued a case is. Between these are the social sciences which have adapted much of the scientific method and applied it to different and less predictable types of data. Claims in social sciences are often based on statistical analysis of probabilities. Alongside such a linear continuum are the applied disciplines that rest on science, social science or humanities foundations but are practical in their orientation.

While we cannot definitively categorise the types of knowledge that disciplines represent, we do know that different approaches to what constitutes knowledge in a subject area are usually implicit rather than explicit. As a disciplinary specialist you are *per se* an insider and know how to express disciplinary values in your writing. To be successful students too need to understand disciplinary knowledge *and* its influence on disciplinary writing.

Does the idea of a cline from the hard sciences to the soft humanities mesh with your view of your discipline? Would this be a useful construct to share with your students? Would you place your discipline in roughly the same place on the continuum as your students would?

In the next section we deal with examples of writing from the science end of the continuum where the types of texts students write are relatively tightly constrained. Such text types, however, are not restricted to science and the ideas discussed have wider relevance.

WRITING PROJECT PROPOSALS AND EXPERIMENTAL REPORTS: EXAMPLES FROM SCIENCE

> For scientific writing to permit the close and independent scrutiny required by the scientific community, it must be both clearly written and easily read. Successful scientific writing therefore, is centred on the reader. To this end, it helps to look at scientific writing as both a product and a process – the production of highly structured documents through a systematised process.
>
> (Goldbort, 2001: 22)

Goldbort's introduction to a new regular feature on effective writing in the *Journal of Environmental Health* highlights the 'highly structured' nature of much scientific writing. Writing in science is characterised by rigid expectations of particular text types. For example, the majority of scientific research articles follow the pattern below with only minor variations (based on Valiela, 2001: 131).

1	Title	6	Results
2	Authors	7	Discussion
3	Abstract	8	Acknowledgements
4	Introduction	9	References
5	Methods	10	Appendices

Research articles emphasise a clear line from recognising a gap in the understanding of some aspect of the natural world (introduction), through setting up an experiment and interpreting the results as filling that knowledge gap (methods and results, and discussion). There is little or no space in this type of writing for serendipity, the chance discoveries, or the discussion of blind alleys or alternative plausible research directions that are often the real social context in which research takes place. Many students need help in both understanding the conventions of science genres and in recognising them as disciplinary artefacts and not merely recounts of how something was achieved. Instead of providing a list of sections to be included in a scientific paper, we feel it is more helpful to indicate to students the functions of different sections and what should go into them.

In Chapter 2 we outlined the functional stages of the project report text type. In Activity 3.1 we go to an earlier part of the project process, writing the project proposal. Below is the outline of the stages of a research proposal for a scientific study. What goes into each stage is elaborated in the description.

Activity 3.1 Functional stages of the scientific project proposal

Functional stage	Description
Title	This stage is a concise but accurate indication of what the project will be about, what is to be measured/investigated and how.
Introduction	Here the aim of your experiment(s) and the theoretical background is indicated. This will normally include a review of literature on what is known about the particular topic and how to investigate it. Indicating where there is a gap in knowledge or investigative procedures provides the rationale for the project.
Materials and methodology	This stage should begin with a list of materials and apparatus to be used. Diagrams to show how the experiment(s) will be set up may be useful. The methodology will have to demonstrate how the aims will be met within constraints on laboratory time, equipment and material. It should be very detailed in order to allow critical evaluation. The conclusions reached can only be considered valid if the research methodology is judged to be sound.
Methods of analysis	This section should show that you have considered what data you will have obtained and how you can best analyse it. If there are different statistical or other analytical techniques available, an evaluation should be given in order to justify your choice.
References	List all the sources referred to in the proposal. This shows what you have read and allows other people to find the sources if they need to.

Academic writing around the research process also includes keeping a laboratory notebook, doing calculations, calculating errors, plotting graphs and finally report writing. In addition to giving the functional stages of the report you can also remind students about specific aspects of report writing that are commonly omitted or mishandled. Figure 3.3 gives an example of advice for writing reports on scientific experiments, but the idea of such tips can be adapted for any discipline.

Figure 3.3 Tips for writing reports on scientific experiments

1   Preface your report with a short abstract.
2   Do not repeat obvious details and theoretical derivations that may be given as a background in the laboratory manual; just refer to them.
3   Mention all precautions and checks – you cannot get credit for them otherwise.
4   Discuss assumption, approximations, consistency of readings, random and systematic errors, limitations of apparatus, suggestions for improvements, abnormal behaviour, comparison of result with that expected, etc.
5   Draw well-labelled diagrams of apparatus. Drawings of specimens should be done initially at least in pencil, and should be large. Where necessary, you should indicate the scale.
6   Refer in the text to all tables and figures.
7   Every physical quantity calculated should have a unit, the correct number of significant figures, and an estimated error.
8   End your report with a brief summary of the conclusions you have reached from the experiment.

(Penz and Shott, 1988: 70)

If you are working with international students, or students who are less familiar with basic features of scientific writing, you can draw out the significant features and how they are expressed by comparing example texts. This is a useful prewriting activity which can be applied to many different text types.

Figure 3.4 shows an exercise written by an English language specialist as a result of collaboration with a discipline specialist.[3] It contains two texts from an experiment to determine the density of a steel cylinder from its mass and diameter. Text A is part of the instructions given prior to carrying out an experiment. Text B is part of the procedure section of the final report. You can use parallel texts like this to get students focusing on differences.

Although the examples given here have been from science, which is the strictest disciplinary area in terms of writing structures, there is considerable overlap with other disciplines. Laboratory reports in psychology, for example, follow the same patterns as those in the sciences. In all cases the overt rhetorical purpose is to recount research experiments and results. A more hidden purpose, however, is seeking to persuade the reader of the validity of the report or claims.

Figure 3.4 Comparing similar texts

Text A – Instructions

Mass of the cylinder

Determine the mass (m) of the steel cylinder using the balance and weights provided. First find the zero reading, that is the mass (m_z) which must be put into the right-hand pan to bring the pointer to zero when the left-hand pan is empty (it may be + or –). Then put the cylinder in the left pan and put weights into the right pan to bring the pointer to zero and obtain the apparent mass (m_a). Calculate the mass of the cylinder using the formula $m = m_a - m_z$.

   NB Take care of the weights, lift them with the forceps and not the fingers, and always replace them in the proper receptacles immediately after use. Leave the pans clean and the beam supported off its knife-edges. The beam should rest on the knife edges only during the actual process of weighing and *not* when changing weights. The pointer reads zero when it swings an equal distance to either side of zero; it should *not* be stationary.

Text B – Procedure section

First the zero reading (m_z) of the balance was found. Then the cylinder was put in the left pan and weights added to the right pan to obtain the apparent mass (m_a). The smallest weight used was 0.01g. Readings were taken with the pointer swinging slightly to avoid frictional effects.

In undertaking the comparison students are learning to identify common practices in writing procedure sections, such as:

- include only the most important steps
- only summarise briefly the precautions given in the instruction
- do not refer to the person doing the experiment
- do not include instructions about calculations
- give additional information if necessary to explain why certain steps were followed.

   As a follow-up activity ask students individually or in pairs to read another set of instructions and write a succinct procedure section.

REPRESENTING DATA AND DISCIPLINE-SPECIFIC TERMINOLOGY: EXAMPLES FROM THE SOCIAL SCIENCES

Earlier we characterised most university disciplines as lying on a continuum from the sciences to the humanities. The writings and practices of social sciences are often characterised as a hybrid of the social – the humanities – and the scientific (Wignell, 1998: 298). Writing practices in the social sciences can therefore share characteristics with both the sciences, for example the use of quantitative data and statistical analysis, and the humanities, for example the use of text types such as the essay. This mixture is reflected in the discipline of geography, which in some institutions is classified as both a humanities and a science subject. We use geography here as a useful exemplar of a discipline straddling the old science-arts boundaries.[4] We look at two key features of texts in geography and social sciences more generally – first, *multimodality*, that is, the combining of text with tables, diagrams and maps, and second, the use of discipline-specific terminology.

Writing multimodal texts: using illustrative material

The main text types written by undergraduate social sciences students are the essay and the project report; both, along with other written tasks, may feature quantitative data. These data may be the result of experiments and physical measurements or the compilation of economic and social statistics, and appear in texts in the forms of tables, graphs and maps. Such data do not necessarily have a specific location; instead, they are tied closely, physically and rhetorically, to the arguments or theories being discussed. Students often need guidance in learning how to set out numerical or pictorial data, understanding how to incorporate them, and knowing when they are appropriate or necessary.

In many disciplines the use of visual representations of data or processes is common. Maps allow detailed information to be depicted in relation to particular places in an efficient way. Tables of figures allow the inclusion of data about which assertions are made. Students have seen such integration of text and visual material in school textbooks where photographs, line drawings, graphs and tables are used. At university level they must learn to reproduce or create a variety of visuals in order to support their written texts. They can benefit from advice ranging from choosing and using suitable software packages to discussing the role of illustrative material as evidence in essays or reports.

You can encourage students to make more than a passing reference to visuals by highlighting the functions they fulfil and the conventions

Figure 3.5 Guidance on using illustrative material

Graphs, pie charts, tables, schematic diagrams, photos and maps are often used to make points more clearly, effectively or succinctly than they can be made in words.

- They supplement rather than duplicate text.

- They must be relevant and discussed in the text.

- Figures and tables should be located as close as possible to the point in the text at which they are discussed and not generally in appendices.

- Graphs, diagrams and maps should be referred to as 'Figures'. Tables and word charts are referred to as 'Tables' and photographs as 'Plates'.

- Illustrative material should be large, comprehensible and self-contained, legible, customised to your work (re-drawn if necessary), correctly identified with sequential Arabic numerals, and correctly attributed if appropriate.

- Titles should specify the subject of the illustration, its location, and the time period to which it refers (e.g. Vietnamese-born population as percentage of total population, Adelaide Statistical Division, 1996).

- Maps and diagrams should have a complete and comprehensive key.

- Labelling should be neat, legible, and relevant to the message being conveyed.

they embody. Figure 3.5 illustrates how this was done for geography and environmental science students.[5]

As well as guidelines such as those in Figure 3.5, you can also integrate discussion directly into your work with students. Activity 3.2 is an example of a short tutorial activity to critically discuss the use of a graph.

Discipline-specific registers

An important aspect distinguishing academic writing in different disciplines is the choice of register and particularly the choice of certain vocabulary. Both the sciences and social sciences make considerable use of specialised terminology, often to develop classification systems with which to describe and explain the world. Some of this terminology may overlap with words in common usage or may be used in other disciplines but some is discipline-specific. Making sure that terminology is clearly understood is often a concern for us as markers of students' work either because the terms themselves embody difficult concepts, or because they are open to different interpretations. If you require students to define or explain terms make this requirement explicit and provide examples of how to do this. An

Activity 3.2 Tutorial examining the use of a graph

Look at the text extract and bar chart and consider these questions.

1   Is there too much or too little detail on the graph?
2   Are the information sources clear?
3   What conclusions can be drawn from the graph?
4   Will the inclusion of the graph support the points being made in the text?
5   Is the graph too complex or too simplistic as a representation of the data?
6   Would a different form of graph or other illustration have been more appropriate?

The marginally higher rate of suicides in rural areas (see Figure 1) is associated with the easy availability of firearms. The necessity of killing vermin and predators on farms means that guns are an obvious choice for the suicidal and are associated most often with male suicides.

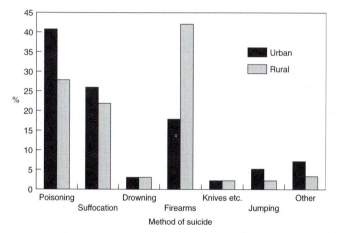

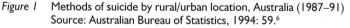

Figure 1   Methods of suicide by rural/urban location, Australia (1987–91)
Source: Australian Bureau of Statistics, 1994: 59.[6]

There are a number of points that students may note in this example.

*   The information in the graph is clearly displayed, including labelling on both the axes, a key and title.
*   The origin of the statistics on which the graph is based is specified.
*   The graph is referred to in the text.
*   It supports the point on differences between rural–urban suicide rates.
*   It does not directly justify the reasoning about the easier availability of firearms in rural areas, nor is there any information about a male–female difference in methods of suicide. These points would need supporting with other evidence.

Activity 3.3 Defining and classifying using discipline-specific language

Geographers frequently discuss both physical and human features in terms of classifications, as in the example of rock types below.

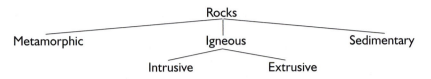

Using Extracts A and B below:

1   Draw a classification system for *weathering* and *communal housing*.
2   In groups consider why these writers have chosen to define and classify these features.

Extract A

Sparks (1986) defines weathering as 'The mechanical fracturing or chemical decomposition of rocks in situ by natural agents at the surface of the earth'. However, a distinction can be drawn between 'normal' and accelerated' rates of weathering (Cooke and Doornkamp, 1990).

Extract B

A major challenge facing contemporary industrial societies is how, and by what means, to construct appropriate housing arrangements to meet the needs and demands of the dependent ageing population (Tinker, 1992). One response has been the development of a variety of forms of *communal housing*. This is a broad term which encompasses a diversity of housing types which are specially designed to accommodate a group of elderly people, living together and sharing a number of communal facilities. The two most significant types of communal housing for the elderly are *sheltered homes* and *residential care homes*.

It is important to recognise, however, that the above definition is somewhat arbitrary, largely due to the existence of varying levels of communalism. First, not all forms of sheltered housing and residential care cater specifically for the elderly. For example, the Registered Homes Act 1984 defined residential care as 'any establishment which provides or is intended to provide residential accommodation with both board and personal care for four or more persons in need of personal care by reasons of old age, disablement, past or present dependence on alcohol or drugs, or past or present mental disorder' (quoted in Sinclair, 1988: 243). Second, the term *residential care* actually incorporates other forms of communal housing such as psychiatric homes and nursing homes. Finally, not all sheltered housing schemes can be classified as communal, because some schemes cater for just one elderly person.

In Extract A, a definition is quoted from a published source, but this is only used as a starting point as the student indicates that greater clarity is achieved by distinguishing different types of weathering. The writer then focuses on just one form of weathering, classifying it in greater detail. In Extract B, the student is careful to specify the meanings of certain terms in the context of the discipline, geography. These terms in common use might well be defined differently in other disciplines.

---

example of modelling defining strategies and extracting classifications from texts is given in the form of a discussion in Activity 3.3.

This discussion of the social sciences has drawn on aspects of writing in geography which come from both social and scientific backgrounds. The use of technical language and classification systems is similar to that found in sciences such as biology and geology. Defining and classifying take place mainly within the argument essay, a text type originally associated most strongly with the humanities. Writing in the social sciences can therefore be described as a hybrid form using the argument essay but containing classificatory systems of organisation and visual and numeric illustrations and data which are associated with sciences. If you are working in the social sciences, you might consider how well your students are coping with combining practices from the sciences and the humanities to create the types of texts required in your discipline, particularly if their background is predominantly *either* science *or* humanities.

WRITING AN ESSAY: AN EXAMPLE FROM THE HUMANITIES

Writing an essay is a widespread form of assessment particularly in the humanities and social sciences. However, as Chapter 2 discussed, *essay* can be a misleading term in that it covers a wide variety of purposes. Typically, according to the discipline area, a lecturer, when asking students to write an essay, has a particular purpose in mind. For example, in English, students may be required to interpret the 'message' or themes of a literary text and support their interpretation through reference to the text as well as to literary critics. In history, on the other hand, students are frequently expected to evaluate the plausibility of an interpretation of past events and to draw on documentary sources as evidence for their argument.

Activity 3.4 What makes an argument essay persuasive?

When you are asked to write an argument essay, lecturers in different disciplines may expect you to do things differently. In history what do you think the expectations are?

Answering the following questions will help you to think this through. In some cases you may want to modify an answer or tick more than one response.

1   When do you make clear your own point of view?
   (a)   at the beginning of the essay
   (b)   at the end of the essay
   (c)   You don't need to have your own point of view.
2   How do you express your point of view?
   (a)   explicitly by using expressions such as *I think, in my view, in my opinion*, etc.
   (b)   implicitly by using expressions such as *it can therefore be argued that, from the evidence it is clear that x is a plausible interpretation, an analysis of the evidence above shows that*, etc.
   (c)   a combination of (a) and (b).
3   Do you need to incorporate other points of view into your essay?
   (a)   No, because that will weaken your own argument.
   (b)   Yes, you need to present an even, balanced presentation of different points of view or perspectives.
   (c)   You need to incorporate points of view that differ from your own in order to avoid making your argument too simplistic. However, counter-arguments need to be weakened where they may undermine your own position.
4   What kind of evidence do you need to draw on to support your arguments?
   (a)   citing expert voices
   (b)   referring to quantitative data
   (c)   drawing on your personal or professional experience
   (d)   documentary evidence
   (e)   referring to qualitative data
   (f)   incorporating pieces of literary texts (e.g. books, poems).
5   How should evidence be used?
   (a)   It must be selected in relation to the sub-arguments and counter-arguments.
   (b)   It must be explicitly linked to the sub-arguments and overall argument (e.g. *The evidence above strongly suggests that ... Rowley's (2001) analysis shows how important x is*).
   (c)   It must be critically analysed.
   (d)   It must carry authority within the field.
   (e)   You need to develop a stance on the evidence e.g. *Doyle claims that* (where claim weakens the evidence) as opposed to *Doyle shows that* (where the stance is relatively neutral).

6   What makes an argument essay convincing?
   (a) selection of evidence
   (b) length of the argument
   (c) how neutral you are in terms of selecting evidence and presenting all points of view.
   (d) acknowledging alternative points of view
   (e) not acknowledging alternative points of view
7   What should the overall style of an argument essay be?
   (a) You should sound authoritative and adopt the voice of a professional historian.
   (b) You should communicate your own personal identity and 'voice'.

Despite these differences, essays typically require a form of argumentation in which the student is expected to put forward an overall argument or point of view and then 'prove' the argument by drawing on supporting evidence. In Chapter 2 one type of argument structure was considered. In this section, we extend our discussion of what we mean by *the argument essay* by considering additional ways of 'building a case'. In particular we draw attention to how writing an argument can vary not only across the major disciplinary areas but within the humanities themselves. Thus, whilst drawing on history to exemplify our points, we suggest strategies for raising students' awareness of how argument essays function differently in different discipline areas.

As a starting point, the awareness-raising task in Activity 3.4 could be used with your students as a means of generating a discussion about the kinds of written argument strategies that are valued within your discipline area.

Responding to and discussing the questions in Activity 3.4 will highlight the different ways in which disciplines favour different forms of argumentation. For example, with regard to forms of evidence, whereas history students typically cite the views of expert historians and draw on primary and secondary sources,[7] English students generally incorporate sections of literary text to support their points of view. Beyond the humanities, evidence frequently includes quantitative data. In the social sciences for example, we saw in the previous section how graphs and statistical findings may be integrated into students' arguments.

In relation to text structure, argument essays are often organised in one of three ways. Figure 3.6 shows the functional stages of each type. The structure referred to as *exposition* was introduced in Chapter 2. As discussed there, a writer may initiate an argument essay by stating a

Figure 3.6 Three ways of structuring an argument essay

Argument structure	Exposition	Discussion	Challenge
Rhetorical purpose	To put forward a point of view or argument	To argue the case for two or more points of view about an issue	To argue against a point of view or argument
Functional stages	Background	Background	Background
	Overall position/ argument	Issue	Position challenged
	Sub-arguments and supporting evidence (counter-arguments)	Sub-arguments and supporting evidence	Rebuttal of sub-arguments and supporting evidence
	Reinforcement of overall position/ argument	Overall position/ argument	Overall position/ argument

position and then put forward a series of arguments and evidence which generally supports the position. Counter-arguments and evidence may be acknowledged so that the writer does not appear overly simplistic or polemical. (Because the counter-argument stage is not obligatory it is placed in brackets.) The writer reinforces the position in the final stage.

The starting point of a *discussion*, on the other hand, is a controversial issue. The writer explores the issue from two or more perspectives before reaching a position in the concluding section. The starting point of a *challenge* is to state the position which will be argued against. A series of rebuttal arguments and supporting evidence then follow. Finally, the writer puts forward the overall argument or position.

Although some disciplines may favour one argumentative structure over another, the three structures shown in Figure 3.6 – exposition, discussion or challenge – commonly occur across the humanities and the social sciences. They may also occur within the applied disciplines, particularly in areas such as education and business studies. It is more in relation to forms of evidence and register that disciplinary variation emerges. If the argument essay is a text type that your students are required to produce, it may be interesting to consider whether they tend to produce expositions, discussions or challenges and whether you respond more favourably to one type rather than another.

As a means of making argument structures explicit and showing how each functional stage contributes to the overall rhetorical purpose, we have analysed a student essay below. We have only taken the main sections of the essay. However, you may like to apply the framework to carry out a comprehensive analysis of an argument essay in your discipline. For example, you could analyse one of your student's essays or a model essay you have written. Using an overhead projector, the structure of the argument could be discussed and evaluated as part of a lecture or tutorial. It may also prove helpful to illustrate how a less successful argument has been structured. Very often, for example, the main argument is unclear or the relationship between it and the sub-arguments and evidence is not obvious. Drawing arrows to show relationships (or their absence) is a concrete way of showing students what is meant by *coherent, relevant, logical,* terms that otherwise may remain elusive.

In the sample abridged (successful) argument essay (Figure 3.7), the stages are labelled in italic face (e.g. *overall argument, sub-argument*) and arrows show how the different stages of the essay link together. For example, the first arrow shows how sub-argument 1 (that personalities in France played an important role in shaping the revolution) directly relates to the overall position (that personalities in France and Russia were more influential in determining revolution than were ideologies).

As you read the essay also consider the types of evidence the history student draws on and the ways in which these compare to the forms of evidence typical in your discipline. The essay was written in response to the question:

> Revolutions are shaped more by dominant personalities than by ideological considerations.
> How far does your study of revolutions show this to be the case?
> In your answer refer to revolutions in:
> Either France and Russia
> or
> China and Cuba

Incorporating evidence into an argument essay

The sample history essay exemplifies the way in which history students can draw on an exposition text structure to debate complex historical

Figure 3.7 Arguments and evidence in an abridged history essay (New South Wales Board of Studies, 1991: 82)

Overall argument/position

It is clear that the course of revolutions is determined more by the behaviour and actions of personalities at the head of the revolutions, rather than by a set of ideologies. Revolutions are also shaped by the actions of social groups who are led or opposed by these personalities. The influence of personalities in both France and Russia overshadowed the numerous, sometimes abandoned ideologies of those two revolutions.

Sub-argument 1

In France, the influence of personalities such as Robespierre and later Napoleon had a large impact on shaping the revolution. Whilst the events of 1789 were caused to a large extent by the frustration of the peasants and sans-culottes, the actions of the leading revolutionaries once power was established was crucial to the outcome of the revolution.

Counter-argument 1 and evidence

W. Doyle (Oxford History of the French Revolution) claims that the influence of the population at the Bastille was most important. Doyle states that the people were convinced that they had saved the National Assembly on July 14th...

Evidence for sub-argument 1

The actions of these two dominant personalities of the French Revolution over-shadowed the ideology of the Revolution, symbolised in the declaration of the Rights of Man and the Citizen in August 1789. Doyle shows that even Robespierre's reliance on his ideology of Virtue, as derived from the writing of Rousseau, was perverted in the end...

Sub-argument 2

Ideology in the USSR also seemed to be overshadowed by the presence of dominant personalities such as Lenin, Trotsky and Stalin, who were willing to abandon their ideology in order to keep alive the Socialist experiment...

Evidence for sub-argument 2

Stalin was perhaps the most dominant personality in the history of the USSR. D. Christian describes his 'great retreat' away from ideals, characterised by the new working-class elite and nomenclature. Stalin's increasing reliance on traditional military discipline was a result of his own personality. The Terror of the purges from 1936–38, claims T. Skocpol (Stalin and Social Revolution), was used to establish and maintain Stalin's own personal dictatorship...

Reinforcement of position/overall argument

In both France and Russia, the dominant personalities of the two revolutions had a much larger influence in shaping the revolutions than revolutionary ideologies, primarily because the survival of both revolutions depended on the temporary casting off or destruction of existing ideological considerations.

interpretations. As we have emphasised, such a structure is not unique to history or the humanities. Nevertheless, despite the commonality of argument structure, the basis on which the student persuades the reader of the validity of the argument – the evidence, in other words – is noticeably different to that of, for example, geography. This point raises the question of how to help students produce an effective argument not only in terms of overall structural organisation but also in terms of integrating evidence which is appropriate and persuasive within a particular disciplinary context. One possible strategy is illustrated in Activity 3.5. It could be adapted for any disciplinary context. In Part 1 of the activity students examine the importance of secondary sources in strengthening an historical argument. In Part 2, the aim is to draw students' attention to the way in which words and phrases referring to historical sources can fall along a continuum of *less endorsing* to *more endorsing* terms (Figure 3.8). Their different choices can be discussed in this light. The activity heightens students' consciousness of the need to interpret and develop a stance on the evidence referred to and how this can be achieved subtly through choice of verbs and other referencing phrases. Although in this book we do not have space to reproduce the entire essay, in your own teaching context, you may want to use two complete essays for each part of the activity. It would also be important to choose essays addressing the disciplinary knowledge and issues that are relevant to the particular group of students.

Illustrated in Activity 3.5 is a text-based approach to teaching disciplinary forms of written argumentation. Alongside an exploration of disciplinary content, the approach emphasises understanding how different linguistic forms at the level of text structure (e.g. choice of argument structure) and register (e.g. choice of words and phrases) actively shape and create interpretations of knowledge rather than merely carrying content. Although in theory such an approach could be applied to all discipline areas, it requires decisions to be made about which written text types play a key role in a specific discipline. It also requires linguistic analysis of the selected text types as a means of making explicit the way knowledge is organised and represents the beliefs of the disciplinary community.

Activity 3.5 Developing a stance on evidence

Part 1

Read the argument essay below. It was written by a student, under exam conditions, in response to the question: *Revolutions are shaped more by dominant personalities than by ideological considerations. How far does your study of revolutions show this to be the case?* Then read it again and underline all the references that the writer makes to secondary sources as we have done in the first two examples. For each reference decide how the source is supporting or countering the writer's main argument.

> It is clear that the course of revolutions is determined more by the behaviour and actions of personalities at the head of the revolutions, rather than by a set of ideologies. Revolutions are also shaped by the actions of social groups who are led or opposed by these personalities. The influence of personalities in both France and Russia overshadowed the numerous, sometimes abandoned ideologies of those two revolutions.
>
> In France, the influence of personalities such as Robespierre and later Napoleon had a large impact on shaping the revolution. Whilst the events of 1789 were caused to a large extent by the frustration of the peasants and sans-culottes, the actions of the leading revolutionaries once power was established was crucial to the outcome of the revolution.
>
> W. Doyle (*Oxford History of the French Revolution*) claims that the influence of the population at the Bastille was most important. Doyle states that the people were convinced that they had saved the National Assembly on July 14th …
>
> The actions of these two dominant personalities of the French Revolution overshadowed the ideology of the Revolution, symbolised in the declaration of the Rights of Man and the Citizen in August 1789. Doyle shows that even Robespierre's reliance on his ideology of Virtue, as derived from the writing of Rousseau, was perverted in the end …

Part 2

Read the next few sections from the student's essay on revolutionary influences. You will notice that a number of words/phrases have been blanked out. These missing words and phrases all refer to, and integrate, primary and secondary sources. Fill in the blanks by choosing appropriate words and phrases. Your choices should strengthen the overall argument. You may wish to look at, and choose from, the words and phrases in Figure 3.8. (Note, however, that the precise meaning of these terms may be dependent on the context.) Some phrases have been completed as a guide.

> Ideology in the USSR also seemed to be overshadowed by the presence of dominant personalities such as Lenin, Trotsky and Stalin, who were willing to abandon their ideology in order to keep alive the Socialist experiment.

Much of Lenin's success in 1917 can be attributed to, as S. Smith (Red Petrograd: Revolution in the Factories 1917) (points out), his 'Bread, land, peace' programme of the April Theses. However, upon ascension to power in October of that year, the Bolsheviks realised that they had to substitute their ideology for pragmatism if they were to defeat the counter-revolutionaries and Interventionists from 1917–20. D. Christian (Power and Privilege) (claims) that Lenin's personality and leadership were most responsible for the success of the Bolsheviks in the Civil War. The need for a new coercive machinery during this period was granted by the implementation of the CHEKA, which, ... S. Fitzpatrick (The Russian Revolution), was the first instrument of the terror. Although the use of terror was in opposition to Marxist ideology on the overuse of coercion, it was leaders such as Trotsky who were able to channel Terror into Red Army victories. (His execution of commissars is the prime example.) A. Ulam (A History of Soviet Russia) (states most clearly) the Bolsheviks' abandoning of their ideology for the need for strong leadership by the dominant personalities of Trotsky and Lenin. Ulam . . . . that the Bolsheviks had to abandon their 'millenarian expectations' and that their democratic scruples atrophied during the tenacious struggle to maintain power.

Stalin was perhaps the most dominant personality in the history of the USSR. Christian . . . . his 'great retreat' away from ideals, characterised by the new working-class elite and nomenclature. Stalin's increasing reliance on traditional military discipline was a result of his own personality. The Terror of the purges from 1936–38, ... T. Skocpol (Stalin and Social Revolution), was used to establish and maintain Stalin's own personal dictatorship.

Opposed to the dominance of personalities in the USSR was the lack of influence of ideology. Christian . . . . that war communism was disastrous, because it represented a mixture of ideology and pragmatism. Apart from the abandoning of ideology during the Civil War years, Ulam . . . . the rehabilitation of the profit motive by NEP in 1921 as proof of the Bolsheviks' perversion of their own ideological considerations. The era of Stalin was also marked by perversion and in some cases destruction of existing Soviet ideology. Skocpol . . . . Stalin's denouncement of the 'petty bourgeois egalitarianism' of equal wages, whilst Christian . . . . the allowing of the 'Sobor' in 1943 as another about-face, this time over the question of religious freedoms.

In both France and Russia, the dominant personalities of the two revolutions had a much larger influence in shaping the revolutions than revolutionary ideologies, primarily because the survival of both revolutions depended on the temporary casting off or destruction of existing ideological considerations.

Figure 3.8 A continuum of less endorsing to more endorsing terms for referring to
        sources

less endorsing	⟶	more endorsing
claim	comment	affirms
contend	say	confirms
suggest	report	agree
argue	state	concur
in x's opinion	declare	make clear
believe	point out	maintain
think	announce	
reckon	cite	
assume	note	
presume	observe	
speculate	write	
x goes so far as to	tell	
suggest that	describe	
propose	put forward	
	explain	
	make the point	
	postulate	
	theorise	
	posit	
	predict	
	see	
	in the view of	
	according to	

To what extent do you feel such an approach is practical in your discipline area?
What would be the advantages of adopting some of the techniques illustrated?
What might be some of the difficulties? Are there departments or centres in your
institution that might provide support for developing such an approach?

WRITING A CASE STUDY: AN EXAMPLE FROM BUSINESS STUDIES

Having looked at some of the key language features that distinguish
writing in science, the social sciences and the humanities, we now turn
to applied disciplines and explore how written texts in this domain reflect
different ways of building and shaping knowledge. Although many of
the applied disciplines (such as business studies, law, health and social

welfare) require students to write argument essays, we focus on the *case study* as it is pivotal in fulfilling one of the main purposes of the domain – the integration of theory with professional practice.

So far in this chapter we have explored the prototypical structures of the research project proposal and the argument essay and their role in achieving the purposes of different discipline areas. In history, for example, the overarching goal is to persuade the reader of a particular interpretation of past events. In business studies, as an example of an applied discipline, the goal is rather more complex. Part of this complexity lies in the common requirement that students write for a dual readership: a real-world audience and an academic assessor. Let us take an example of an assignment in business studies:

> Draw on one of the frameworks for analysing business strategy which you have encountered on the course and make an assessment of an organisation you are familiar with. Write a case study to illustrate your findings, and make some recommendations that would be useful to your business colleagues.

These instructions make it clear that students are expected to envisage two audiences: a) the lecturer who will assess their work; and b) real or imagined business colleagues.

The assessment task requires students to apply theoretical knowledge (i.e. an understanding of an analytic framework) to a professional situation. Therefore the underlying educational rationale for the assignment is twofold – to assess students' understanding of disciplinary theory and to evaluate their ability to put theory to practical use in a manner that is accessible to – and appropriate for – business colleagues. Not surprisingly, the degree to which both these aspects are assessed and the weighting attached to each dimension is not straightforward. This issue is discussed in greater detail in Chapter 4. Here we focus on the linguistic features and strategies that students need to control to produce a successful response.

First, let us consider the overall structure of a written case study. Though *case study* is, like *essay*, a rather imprecise term and includes a number of different forms of writing each with a distinct structure, in broad terms, its overall rhetorical purpose can be described as *reporting on research and arguing a case*. Generally, the case study consists of four main functional stages:

Background
Analytical Framework/Approach to Study
Findings
Implications for professional practice
(Recommendations – optional)

Figure 3.9 provides students with an explanation of each of the stages, highlighting problem areas. You might use this resource with your students as a means of reflecting on the difficulties of writing a case study. You may also adapt it to capture the kind of structure that you would expect from students writing up a case study in your discipline.

Having considered how far the functional stages outlined in Figure 3.9 match those of case studies that you are familiar with, three questions to contemplate here are:

- What kinds of tension are students likely to experience when writing for two distinct audiences?
- What might be the consequences for both the text structure and register?
- What types of teaching strategy could help students resolve such issues?

Raising awareness of professional and academic styles of writing

Asking students to shape information in order to meet, simultaneously, the conventions of the academic and the business (or professional) community often leads to unsatisfactory assignments that fail to meet the expectations and conventions of either audience (Hewings, 1999b). In this section we explore strategies for raising students' awareness of the role that language plays in managing the needs of a dual readership. In particular we look at ways of avoiding an overly personal and anecdotal style when drawing on professional experience.

One helpful strategy is for students to compare the styles of different types of journal article. This is a particularly valuable exercise in postgraduate programmes where students are frequently encouraged to read both journals aimed at practitioners and journals whose primary audience is academics. Whereas the former tend to employ a personal and engaging style (particularly in contexts such as business), the latter follow more traditional academic conventions of presenting objective and impersonal accounts. Thus, aside from the actual design of assessment

Figure 3.9 The functional stages of a case study

Functional Stages	Description
Background	In this stage the area of the organisation/professional situation that would benefit from closer analysis is outlined. A broader context for the study may need to be provided in that the marker (the lecturer as opposed to colleagues) may not be familiar with the organisation/professional situation featured (e.g. its structure, goals and culture).
Analytical Framework or Approach to Study	One of two stages are chosen at this point, depending on how far the text is oriented towards the 'academic assessor' as opposed to the 'business colleague/professional audience'. If the latter, approach to study is the appropriate stage. In this functional stage, the theoretical approach is explained in non-technical terms and is made meaningful to a professional as well as an academic audience. If writing primarily for an academic assessor, analytical framework is the appropriate stage. This stage provides a detailed explanation of, and rationale for, the selected framework of analysis.
Findings	In this stage the main findings of the application of a theoretical model to a professional situation are highlighted.
Implications for Organisation	The goal in this section is to interpret the findings particularly in terms of the insights they provide into the aspect of the organisation/profession under focus.
Recommendations	The overall function of this stage is to put forward suggested action points based on an assessment of the situation arising from the interpretation of the information collected.

tasks, the kinds of writing students are exposed to, and which they often perceive as exemplary writing, may lead them to develop a confused style in which academic and professional 'speak' are fused together. Students therefore need guidance in focusing on the kind of relationship developed between writer and reader, the level of formality created and the type of information foregrounded.

Another useful strategy is to ask students to focus on samples of their own personal writing which can then be compared with more formal, rewritten extracts, as in Activity 3.6.

It is important that students understand both the ideological and functional dimensions of the use of first person pronouns (see also the

Activity 3.6 Comparing student voices

Compare the following two pieces of writing.

Extract 1

> 'Corporate philosophy'. What's that? When I heard about this term, I almost screamed. Can a corporation have a philosophy? What does the corporate philosophy stand for?

Extract 2

> 'Corporate philosophy' is a term that needs to be defined in terms of what is meant by philosophy within a corporate environment. I think it is important to debate whether or not a corporation can actually have a philosophy.

In Extract 1, draw students' attention to the way questions are used to develop a dialogic style between writer and reader. Although the reader cannot directly reply to the writer, the use of questions engages the reader and writer in considering the issue together.

The use of first person pronouns, the colloquial use of *that* and *this* and the inclusion of the writer's emotional reaction (*I almost screamed*) contribute to a familiar, personal style. Finally, the inclusion of *I* takes up the prominent first position in two clauses (*When I...* and *I almost...*) and thus draws attention to the student's personal responses and reactions rather than to the topic under discussion.

Extract 2, in contrast, illustrates how the writer's subjective voice can be integrated into a traditional academic style.

section on Register in Chapter 2). Currently, some members of various academic disciplines are beginning to question the way in which writers and researchers – and the subjectivity of their views – have traditionally been made invisible in written texts. In some cases, the explicit and direct intrusion of the writer into the text is a useful reminder that knowledge is mediated by human beings operating in particular historical, cultural and social contexts. On the other hand, it is also useful for students to be aware of how the overuse of *I* or *we* can have a negative effect on the conceptual development of an essay. For instance, the use of *I* may draw attention away from the phenomenon under examination and interrupt the flow of information.

In summary, the applied disciplines make different writing demands than the sciences, social sciences or humanities in that they frequently require students to integrate theoretical frameworks with professional practice. This can create tension in students who may have learned to write effectively for academic and professional audiences but who may face problems in integrating the two styles. We have shown how it is often helpful to provide students with models of writing with contrasting registers. Such models can be used to develop students' awareness of how the use of grammar and vocabulary produces different effects. Students can learn to write with a voice that is more or less personal or impersonal, more or less subjective or objective.

CONCLUSION

This chapter has illustrated a variety of text-based techniques that can be used in the teaching of disciplinary forms of disciplinary writing. Many of the teaching strategies and activities aim to raise students' consciousness of how texts can be structured to achieve the goals of the assessment task (and in a wider sense, the goals of the particular discipline). You will have seen how language choices (such as the use of technical terms or personal pronouns) actively shape and create interpretations of knowledge rather than merely carrying content.

Let us return to the initial scenario where we saw how the move towards greater multi-disciplinarity has caused difficulties for students such as Paul. How might the approaches discussed in this chapter be of use in such a context? Primarily, it can be argued, as Ball *et al.* have (1990: 357), that, as lecturers, we need to be consciously aware of how disciplines are defined by a 'complex and diffuse conjunction of objects, methods, rules, definitions, techniques and tools'. They conclude, as a consequence, that students need to be 'in control of specific field conventions, a set of rules and methods which mark the discourse as belonging to a certain discipline' (Ball *et al.*, 1990: 357).

It seems then that lecturers need to provide students with as much scaffolding and guidance as possible to develop their understanding of how text types and register are central to the ways in which disciplines are distinguished. More importantly students need to be shown how these disciplinary differences are tied to the overall goals of a discipline and its particular traditions and methods.

NOTES

1   Based on a case discussed by Lea and Street, 1998.
2   Text types dealt with explicitly in this chapter are shown in italic.

3   Published in Dudley-Evans, 1985: 20.
4   Physical geographers have traditionally seen themselves as part of the scientific community. Human geography is more problematic, often located within humanities, arts or social sciences faculties.
5   The advice in Figure 3.5 comes from a book written by a geographer, Iain Hay (1996). Discipline-specific advice on aspects such as using diagrams, statistical data and illustrations is often available in specialist books aimed at students, e.g. Penz and Shott, 1988.
6   Graph re-drawn from Hay, 1996: 67.
7   In history, primary sources refer to documentary and other types of evidence produced around the time of an historical event. Secondary sources refer to documents written by historians.

Chapter 4

Planning the assessment of student writing

Contradictory expectations in assessment[1]

A law student wrote an essay that required her to advise two people being charged by the police. The student was concerned because this suggested the addressee for her essay should be her fictitious clients. However, she was not actually advising clients, but writing an academic essay to be marked by a lecturer. Another problem derived from the lecturer's oral instruction to include 'not too many facts and to argue it'. The student interpreted 'argue' as the need to present her clients with one preferred option rather than setting out a range of perspectives, as the question itself seemed to require. She was further confused by generic assessment guidelines that told students:

> Write in the impersonal third person. There are few things so irritating as the constant intrusion of the author via the (unnecessary) first person 'I think ...'.

This guidance seemed to be contradicted when (later) feedback on the student's essay called for 'more evidence of what *you* thought the likely outcome would have been'.

INTRODUCTION

The problems faced by the student above are not uncommon. In producing any form of writing for assessment, students need to work out what type of text they are expected to produce and how this will be evaluated. However, even when instructions or guidelines are given, students may be left uncertain about aspects of the assessment. In this case, the student had difficulty with different forms of guidance, which she felt offered conflicting advice; and also with the term *argue* – perhaps unsurprisingly as the notion of argument is notoriously difficult to pin down (see Chapter 2).

This chapter addresses a number of issues in the assessment of students' writing, including the selection of text types for assessment and the provision of guidance on these to students. We see these as part of a more general strategy for assessing writing – the main question we address is: how can we devise an effective strategy for the assessment of students' writing, so that this satisfies the requirements of a particular course of study and is meaningful to students? More specifically, the chapter aims to explore:

- different purposes for assessing writing and (in the light of these) the question of what should be the focus of assessment
- assignment marking and the value of different types of assessment criteria
- the identification of particular types of writing for assessment
- issues to do with the wording of assignments and assessment guidance
- how students may participate in assessing their own or others' writing
- steps that may be taken to avoid plagiarism.

Aspects of assessment are dealt with further in Chapter 5, which looks at decisions made at the point of assessing, or responding to students' writing: what to focus on when commenting on students' writing, and how to communicate feedback to students. Throughout both chapters we try to take account of the fact that there is no ideal – or, for that matter, self-evident – way of assessing students' writing: what is at issue is the identification of a 'best-fit' strategy given your own teaching context.

ASSESSMENT: PRELIMINARY ISSUES

Earlier chapters have pointed to a number of challenges faced by students in beginning to write academic texts, many of which have implications for assessment. While Chapter 3 focused on the characteristics of student writing in different disciplines, students may have to contend with differences across a range of assessment practices: grading systems, sets of criteria, the forms of guidance (if any) that are available, types of feedback given on writing. Assessment practices are frequently unclear to students (see e.g. Ivanic, 1998; Lea and Street, 1998; Lillis, 1999). Lillis argues that this works particularly against non-traditional students including (in Britain) working-class and Black students, and students who are older than 18 at the beginning of their study: such students are least likely to be familiar with the conventions of academic writing. International students, who may have experience of quite different forms of written assessment, and may have different expectations from those of their teachers, are another group likely to be particularly disadvantaged by unclear assessment practices (McNamara and Harris, 1997).

When devising an assessment strategy, there may be a tension between introducing 'ideal' forms of assessment and minimising potential confusion and misunderstandings for students. For instance, innovative assessment practices may be desirable in their own terms, but they may be unfamiliar to students and inconsistent with practices elsewhere. This tension suggests that innovation needs to be balanced against consistency; that there needs to be continuing dialogue between lecturers on related courses; and that assessment practices require explicit discussion with students.

Purposes of assessment

As a starting point to devising an assessment strategy, it is useful to identify the purposes for which you need to assess students' writing. The list below suggests some examples.

Purposes for assessing students' writing may include:

- to provide evidence of students' knowledge and understanding of a particular course of study
- to provide evidence of students' acquisition of subject-specific skills, or the ability to apply knowledge and understanding (e.g. students' ability to carry out certain forms of analysis)
- to indicate how effectively students can express their knowledge and understanding in writing (e.g. using disciplinary conventions such as those discussed in Chapter 3)
- to help students learn, or consolidate their learning (both of subject knowledge/skills and of academic writing conventions)
- to provide feedback to students on their work
- to motivate students to carry out certain activities
- to provide a diagnostic assessment of a student's writing (before providing writing support for the student)
- to help you evaluate your own teaching
- to help students evaluate their own learning.

Many of the purposes listed here are complementary, and it may not always be possible to separate them. Assessment also has unforeseen outcomes – for instance common problems in the assignments completed by a whole class of students may suggest to a lecturer certain ways in which teaching could be improved. Your own assessment purposes are unlikely to map directly on to those listed above; you may also have different, or additional purposes. The main point, however, is to identify these purposes explicitly as they will affect all aspects of your assessment strategy.

Set against your purposes for assessing students' writing you will probably be aware of a number of constraints that affect both what and how you can assess. These may include policy developments at national or governmental level, as well as institutional purposes for assessment (e.g. the need to 'measure' students, to allocate a certain class of degree or other award, and to ensure comparability of standards). At a more local (e.g. departmental) level there will probably be a need to accommodate, in certain respects, to the practices of other colleagues. In combination, these constraints will ensure that assessment is necessarily a compromise – the point about 'best-fit' that we made above – and not the ideal practice an individual lecturer may wish to see.

Assessment for grading or teaching?

A distinction is commonly made between *formative* and *summative* assessment. Formative assessment would not normally be graded – it has a teaching function, to help students improve their work rather than measure their achievements. Summative assessment, on the other hand, is formally graded. Brown *et al.* (1997) note that formative assessment is still unusual in higher education because of time pressures on lecturers. However, formative assessment may have a number of useful functions. Used for a first assignment, in particular, it can familiarise students with the demands of writing in a new subject area (in a less threatening way than assessment for a grade); it can help you identify students who need more help with their writing, and it can provide a focus for group discussion about the requirements of the course or common patterns of writing problems among students in the class. Because formative assessment is a teaching tool, it should be closely tied in with adequate feedback on students' writing.

While it is possible to have assessment that is purely formative or summative, both elements may also be combined (Brown, 1999). For instance, the same assignment may receive teaching feedback and be awarded a grade. Formative assessment can also be used for the first draft of an assignment, before a final version is produced for summative assessment. Brown stresses the importance of choosing thoughtfully and of thinking about the timing of assessment – formative assessment is of little use at the end of a semester, and for assessment to be useful to students it needs to be incremental. Lecturers may be constrained here by institutional requirements, but if there is some flexibility during the semester it may even be possible for students themselves to decide when they feel ready to be assessed. If students seem unlikely to complete formative assignments because no grade is given, you can consider a summative assignment instead with a low weighting attached to it.

How do you currently balance formative and summative elements in assessment? Are you satisfied with the way this works, or could the balance be shifted? (Note that the section 'Students' participation in assessment' later in this chapter discusses how students may participate in both formative and summative assessment; and Chapter 5 considers the nature of feedback provided in formative assessment.

Assessment criteria

When determining what the focus of assessment should be, it can be difficult in practice to disentangle content (and ideas) in student writing from the way these are expressed. A good starting point is for lecturers to think through at an early stage whether criteria for assessment should be devised. These can help clarify for a lecturer what he or she wants to assess and how. Lecturers can use criteria without showing them to students, but we take the view that assessment should be as transparent as possible, to make expectations explicit. Criteria can simply be given to students, or can be formulated in negotiation with students.

What is the focus of your own assessment of students' writing? For example, do you attempt to separate the assessment of content from students' ability to communicate this effectively? Do you use formal assessment criteria – and if so, how do these guide your marking? We discuss examples of criteria below.

Figure 4.1 Marking criteria on an English language course

Your tutor will primarily make use of the following criteria in deciding what mark to give your assignment:

- *The relevance of your answer to the question as set.*

Your tutor will look for evidence that you have clearly understood the question and directed your answer accordingly.

- *Your knowledge and understanding of the course material.*

Your tutor will look for evidence that you have understood and can draw effectively on research evidence, ideas, concepts and arguments that are central to the course.

- *Your ability to discuss and evaluate alternative explanations and arguments.*

Researchers and other commentators may provide different (and sometimes competing) explanations for linguistic events and processes. Your tutor will look to see whether you are able to discuss these, and evaluate any arguments put forward in support of a particular viewpoint.

- *The ability to present and pursue an argument.*

Your tutor will examine the structure of your answer to assess how well you can put together the material you use to sustain and support an argument.

- *The ability to express yourself clearly using academic conventions as appropriate.*

Your tutor will look for clarity in your work, in the way you make your points, present research finding and make critical comments. You are not expected to make extensive use of technical vocabulary, but you should be able to refer to key terms and concepts from the course materials. You should also acknowledge clearly any sources you have drawn on.

(The Open University, 2002a)

There are several ways in which criteria may be related to marking. Figure 4.1 provides an example of broad marking criteria devised for essays written on an English language course. In this case, the criteria set out what the marker will be looking for, but a single overall grade is allocated to the essay. Figure 4.2 comes from a literature course. Here, criteria are related to particular grading bands (they specify what a student has to do to achieve an 'A' grade, or a 'B' grade, etc.). Figure 4.3 provides an example of weighted criteria. It is possible to allocate weightings to different aspects of writing – e.g. you may wish to weight linguistic accuracy lower than content or text structure. In Figure 4.3, a report for a business studies

Figure 4.2 Grade-related criteria on a literature course

'A' range (88, 95, 100 per cent, 'excellent')

Knowledge of texts: You made an excellent choice of texts and in discussion foregrounded their literary qualities.

Presentation and scholarly methods: Argument and evidence were well woven together and you made consistent use of literary terms. You quoted accurately and provided good references and bibliography.

Argument and response to assignment: Your argument was well controlled and organised and addressed all parts of the topic. Perhaps you used your own insights to extend the argument beyond the terms of the set book.

Understanding of the issues: You clearly understood the issues raised by the assignment and the relevant course material, including seeing why these are important in terms of literary study. Maybe you used your own material from beyond the course.

'B' range (73, 80 per cent, 'good pass')

Knowledge of texts: You made a good choice of texts for discussion, and demonstrated knowledge of them in terms of content and their literary qualities through apt citation and quotation.

Presentation and scholarly methods: Your essay was made up of fluent sentences well organised into paragraphs. You probably made some use of literary terms and provided clear references.

Argument and response to assignment: The essay addressed the issues raised in the assignment thoroughly, in a way that shows you are clearly thinking for yourself. Your argument showed evidence of your having reflected on the topic.

Understanding of the issues: You showed understanding of the issues raised by the course material, particularly in the way you were able to put things in your own words, but most probably you stayed within the bounds of the course material.

(The Open University, 2001)

---

course, the criteria correspond more or less to functional stages in the report, with analysis given a higher weighting than other stages.

Broad and relatively open criteria, such as those in Figure 4.1, give you more flexibility in allocating marks to students' writing, but even where criteria are tied to specific grading bands, or given a specific weighting, markers need to exercise judgement and a certain degree of 'impression marking' is involved. A further reason for discussing or negotiating criteria with students is to make explicit your interpretations of criteria and to attempt to reach a joint understanding of what is valued in students' writing.

Figure 4.3 Weighted criteria from a business studies course

Choose a situation or events that you consider problematic [...]

Write a report on the situation for an appropriate person. The report must include:

(a) a brief description of the situation and/or events and why they are or were problematic *(5 marks)*
(b) an analysis of the situation or events *(20 marks)*
(c) a discussion of possible ways of addressing the situation, or of preventing such a situation arising, or of handling it better in future *(15 marks)*
(d) your conclusions which may be specific proposals for action or reflections on what you have learned from the analysis and its implications for your management practice *(10 marks)*.

Total: 50 marks

(The Open University, 1996)

How do the types of criteria exemplified in Figures 4.1, 4.2 and 4.3 relate to your own practice? Given your current teaching context, what would you see as the strengths and weaknesses of these different types of criteria?

Providing guidance on assessment

In addition to criteria, other forms of guidance can be provided for students, either as written handouts or in the form of structured group exercises or informal discussion about your expectations. Points to consider include:

- What form(s) of guidance do you wish or need to give to students?
- What specific purposes does this need to serve?
- How detailed should guidance be – is there a danger in saying too much? How constrained should students be?
- How far should the guidance be negotiated with students? (We deal with students' participation in assessment below.)

Guidance may be brief and describe only the length and format of assignments required (word count, page numbering, student's name and other details required), with little else except for a list of essay titles to choose from. Guidance can, however, be more detailed and specific, and may include indications of the writing style considered appropriate, referencing conventions, the use of sources (including personal and anecdotal experience), checklists and so on.

The above points have implications for how an assessment strategy is constructed and implemented. We focus in this chapter on writing rather than assessment more generally, but see the annotated bibliography for related or more general issues. We do not deal in this book with more technical aspects of assessment such as norm- and criterion-referencing, different types of grading, or the balance of coursework and examinations (see Brown *et al.*, 1997; Brown and Glasner, 1999; and Knight, 1995 for more on these). We turn now to look at ways in which different types of written assignments can be assessed.

IDENTIFYING WHAT TYPES OF WRITING TO ASSESS

Tasks and text types

A key issue in designing an assessment strategy will be deciding what kinds of tasks you expect students to carry out, and what kinds of texts they will produce as a result. Chapter 3 discussed text types such as the essay, which usually requires students to demonstrate their knowledge and understanding of a particular subject area as well as their ability to represent this using appropriate writing conventions; and the case study, which may incorporate an element of independent research or (in professional courses) the ability to integrate academic theory and professional practice. Essays, case studies and other types of writing such as laboratory reports have become conventional within certain disciplines, but many alternatives are available that provide opportunities for different forms of writing and extend the range of what is assessed. As an example, Figure 4.4 suggests possible alternatives to the essay and the laboratory report. Figure 4.5 gives two examples of essays from mathematics, a subject not usually associated with essay writing.

It's worth thinking about the kinds of writing you usually ask students to produce for assessment: are students producing an appropriate range of writing? Would it be beneficial to extend this range? Or could the range you have be too broad (with inadequate opportunity for students to become very familiar with different text types)?

Figure 4.4 Some alternatives to the essay and the laboratory report

Existing task: Essay	**Existing task: Laboratory report**
Set:	Set:
Article for a serious newspaper	Instructional guide for beginner
Article for professional magazine	Popular account of experiment
Article for a popular newspaper	and its findings
Book review	Brief seminar paper on experiment
Paper to a committee	Group report on a set of linked
Case for an interest group	experiments
Popular book review	
Script for a radio programme	
Script for a TV programme	

(Brown et al., 1997: 45)

Figure 4.5 'Concept essays' from a course on calculus

(a) In your own words, explain how the ideas of differentiation have been extended to apply to functions of two variables and to vector functions of one variable. Take about half a page to a page for each. Use diagrams to help your explanations. Try to explain why the extensions have been done the way you have explained and not some other way. For example, explain why partial derivatives are the central idea for functions of two variables as opposed to, say, finding the slope of the tangent plane.

(b) Summarise, in your own words, in about a page or so, the factors which existed in the seventeenth century which led to the main ideas of calculus being invented at that time.

(Roberts, undated; cited in Toohey, 1999: 177)

Note: 'Concept essays' were fairly short pieces of written work that allowed students to demonstrate their growing understanding of calculus. They were used alongside other forms of assessment that required students to 'do' calculus or apply it in some way.

In practice, the types of writing you ask students to produce will derive from your purposes for assessment, and what you actually wish to assess: for instance, how important is it that students can explain academic concepts or procedures to a lay audience; that they have practice in writing reports; or that they can write persuasively for academic, professional or lay readers?

Whatever types of writing you decide to assess, students will need guidance on these. Chapters 2 and 3 have demonstrated that the conventions of text types such as essays and reports are highly variable (e.g.

they differ between academic areas, between departments and between individual lecturers). Apparently common, everyday texts such as magazine articles are no more transparent. Such texts may actually be more problematical for students because they depend on a mixed, and perhaps confusing notion of audience: while ostensibly written for a popular audience, they are probably being evaluated by an academic lecturer and need to satisfy the requirements of an academic course of study (a similar audience problem was noted by the law student at the beginning of this chapter). Many of the activities in Chapters 2 and 3, designed to help students understand the conventions of academic writing, may be used to explore the kinds of writing students need to produce for assessment. Providing clear assessment criteria and discussing these with students (see earlier discussion in this chapter) should also help students understand the requirements of particular types of assignments.

Activity 4.1 Considering the requirements of an assignment

In order to help students understand more fully the kind of writing they are expected to produce, and how this may be assessed, students may be asked to consider and perhaps mark an (anonymized) sample assignment. Below is an example of such an exercise that was used on an Open University course.

Sample assignment exercise

For whole group

Students are to read sample assignment before the tutorial and jot down: (a) its strengths; (b) where the assignment might be improved. They could be advised to use course assessment criteria for this activity.

At the tutorial, students compare notes (probably in small groups) and see if they can reach agreement, or understand how/why they differ. For this exercise, they should use the assessment criteria. Possibly, each group could focus on different criteria.

In a plenary session – each group reports back. The lecturer can explain how they would evaluate the assignment – again, according to the criteria. The lecturer could expand discussion to include the kinds of things they are looking for, more generally, under each criterion. If it seems helpful, the original marker's comments can be distributed and compared with students' evaluations.

For students who would like more help with assignment writing

With these students, it may be useful to examine assignment in greater detail, focusing on issues that are of particular concern (e.g. what counts as relevant material from all that students could potentially draw on in an assignment; text structure; what makes a good introduction/conclusion; appropriate register).

Assessing journals and other forms of personal writing

Academic writing is often relatively impersonal, but in some courses students may be encouraged to engage in more personal or reflective forms of writing, concerned with the process of learning rather than just the outcome. This could happen within any piece of extended writing including academic essays and reports, but we shall focus here particularly on learning journals as illustrations (see Chapter 2).

A number of issues are raised by the assessment of personal reflection. Assessment constitutes a formal recognition of the value of reflection where this is seen to be important on a course. More practically, assessment may encourage students to engage in reflection or to complete journals, and to take these activities seriously (it is widely recognised that students pay more attention to assessed items than to what lecturers tell them is important – see e.g. Brown *et al.*, 1997). The assessment of reflection is, however, problematical. Figure 4.6 illustrates some concerns raised by students whose journals were an assessed part of their writing on physiotherapy and occupational therapy courses.

Figure 4.6 Students' responses to the assessment of reflective writing

I feel quite wary about actually putting it down in black and white and then handing it in. You feel quite vulnerable.

How do you ascribe a mark to a personal account with any real meaning?

How can someone else decide if it is good or bad?

… and I think it's for assessment purposes. I don't think it's a true reflection of how we reflect.

Those people able to write it down properly might get a better mark but they may not necessarily be more reflective.

(Stewart and Richardson, 2000: 373–4)

Students may feel uncomfortable about their personal reflections being read and evaluated by others. But in this case they also raise concerns about the validity of the assessment process: how does a reader, as an outsider, judge the value of someone else's personal reflection? A related issue has to do with ethical considerations – as suggested by Brown in the following example:

> … a nursing tutor found herself very concerned to be reading an
> account of a student who was working on a geriatric ward nursing

patients dying of cancer, when at home she was caring for her own mother who was dying of cancer. Assessing that particular reflective journal was a harrowing experience, and the tutor concerned found herself questioning the acceptability of what she found to be a rather prurient experience.

(Brown, 1999: 97)

If students acknowledge the assessment process and tailor their writing to meet these demands they will be engaging in a very different activity from personal writing in which they reflect on their learning/experiences for their own benefit. The students in Figure 4.6 suggest that, at the very least, personal reflection will be distorted by assessment.

If you wish to make some assessment of students' writing in reflective journals, an alternative to assessing these directly is to draw on them as evidence in other forms of assessment. The examples in Figure 4.7 come from a course in dentistry in which students' reflections contributed to their self-assessment of their work. This was discussed with lecturers and a final grade was agreed.

Figure 4.7 Extracts from journal entries completed by dentistry students

(1)   This subject has increased my theoretical and clinical knowledge and, more importantly, my self-confidence! I've learned from my mistakes and the constructive criticism of the tutors. I think I'd give myself a Credit/Pass 1. I hope that's on a par with your assessment.

(2)   It's nice to have a tutor in the clinic, having read my evaluation, actually express positive feelings towards me and indicate that he thinks I've got what it takes to become a successful dentist. Not many people really reflect those feelings apart from my family who don't really understand the amount of pressure involved in learning to be a dentist.

(Wetherell and Mullins, 1996: 109)

Students may also quote selectively from journals in assessed work. Brown (1999), for instance, suggests that students may be asked to keep a journal as a private document but select critical incidents to write up for assessment. In this case, students would typically be asked to provide:

- a brief description of the context
- perhaps a brief photocopied extract of a non-sensitive passage from the journal relating to the incident
- a description of what the student as practitioner actually did

- some demonstration of the ways in which theory learned on the course influenced the student's actions
- what alternatives were considered and rejected and why
- how the student would tackle the incident differently on another occasion
- what learning the student took away from the incident and how this would affect future practice.

(Brown, 1999: 98)

Using journals as a source for assessment allows students to draw on personal experience, critically evaluate this and demonstrate what they have learned while also reducing some of the difficulties caused by assessing personal experience directly.

To what extent do you think it would be appropriate to include students' personal reflections on their learning (in journals or other forms of writing) as part of the assessment you make of their writing?

Assessing collaborative writing

We have focused so far on writing produced by individual students, but students may also write more collaboratively (see Chapter 2). While this may be beneficial as a learning activity, it raises problematical issues for assessment: in particular it is difficult (some might say impossible) to make a fair assessment of individual contributions to collaboratively produced writing.

Collaboration may take different forms, ranging from students commenting on drafts of one another's writing but taking responsibility for individual final texts; to jointly authored texts in which responsibility is shared. Assessment may be formative (in which case there is no requirement to distinguish the work of individual students); or summative (where individual grades need at some point to be allocated). It is summative assessment that seems to raise the more important issues.

If your own students write collaboratively, do you assess this and if so, how? What would you see as the benefits and dangers of assessing collaborative writing?

Figure 4.8 provides two accounts of collaboratively produced writing, both of which were summatively assessed. The first example results in a separate grade for each student – although the other student may have contributed to this grade through their comments on drafts. There are clearly issues of fairness here, but one might argue that this is similar to practices in professional academic writing in which colleagues frequently comment on, but take no responsibility for, others' writing. The second example concerns jointly authored writing in which individual students agree to share the same grade. There is inevitably a danger that a grade allocated to the group as a whole may not reflect students' differing contributions to the writing process or the final product, and this may pose problems if students are *required* to submit collaborative writing for assessment. Where students agree (voluntarily) to share a grade this seems more acceptable – again, it is similar to a great deal of professional academic writing where writers agree to take joint responsibility for collaboratively authored papers and books.

Figure 4.8 Collaborative writing produced for assessment

Collaborative work on an education management course

Two students on an education management course planned a joint project that evaluated the introduction of a new management system in their school. The students designed the project together, but each student focused on different aspects of the research. They wrote up separate but linked reports that included, in each case, a reflection on their own participation in the research process. They read and commented on each other's drafts, but each student took responsibility for their own final report, and these were assessed and graded separately.

Collaborative work in science teaching

Three students on an MA course worked as teachers in the same school and together carried out a project that involved developing and evaluating aspects of the science curriculum. The students said all stages of the project would be collaborative and it would be impossible to distinguish their individual contributions. They therefore wanted to produce a jointly authored project report for assessment. Since other students on the course were assessed individually, the three collaborating students were required to carry out a larger project and produce a longer written report. They agreed in advance that they would share the same grade for the report.

Portfolios

A portfolio is a folder of a student's work completed during a course or programme. So far portfolios have not been widely used in British higher education for assessing written assignments. Portfolios have been used in courses where evidence of professional practice is required and the range of tasks undertaken by students is broad. For example in health care or teaching, students may need to present evidence of tasks completed, or issues considered, in the form of reports, checklists and interview data, as well as traditional essays. However, the approach has been used more widely in the United States for writing and some strengths and weaknesses of portfolio assessment emerge. Portfolios can be beneficial in that they allow students to preserve, build upon and improve their writing over time. Students have an ongoing record of their progress, and can include different drafts of their work as evidence of achievement. In some situations, students are asked to select a number of pieces of their best work; in others, all of their work is included to show their development over time. Because of this emphasis on drafts, revisions and feedback, portfolios are one way in which students can be encouraged to assess their own writing and respond to feedback. The work produced can be a more accurate representation of writing tasks which occur in real life, particularly in the workplace. Because of the range of items that portfolios can include, they can provide breadth and depth for academic development. For students who fear or do poorly on time-limited examinations, or for students whose first language is not English, portfolios can replace the necessity of a high-stakes test where performance on a single day can have lifelong consequences.

The disadvantages of portfolios mainly relate to time considerations, for both lecturers and students. More resources are required for assessing portfolios (the whole, as well as the component parts, is often assessed at the end of a module or degree programme). However, as Young (1999) points out, markers soon become familiar with the format as long as there are clear and simple criteria for assessment. Students have to work harder to compile and organise their portfolios, and may be required to produce a piece of writing at the end of their study that reflects on the portfolio's contents – they may therefore resist this additional work, even if they perceive its value.

The box 'Assessment methods and weightings' is an extract from a portfolio assessment strategy on a writing course at the University of

---

Assessment methods and weightings

Students will be required to submit a Writing Portfolio for their module grade. Portfolios, which promote not only writing processes but also writing as a way of thinking and learning, will consist of the following elements and their respective weightings:

- *Essays*: Each student will be required to submit *drafts* of the types of essays examined in this module: (1) Analysis and Interpretation, (2) Describing Processes and (3) Cause and Effect. Drafts will be weighted at 30 per cent. In addition to the drafts, each student will be required to revise and polish ONE essay of their choice from their required SLS modules. The total weighting for the finished essay is 35 per cent.
- *Journals*: Students will be required to maintain reading-response double entry journals throughout the duration of the module. Journals will be weighted at a total of 10 per cent.
- *Reader Responses*: Students must submit one peer response for each of the three essay drafts. Total weight for peer responses is 10 per cent.
- *Exemplative Précis*: The first two required texts are weighted at 5 per cent.
- *Self-Improvement Plan*: Each student will be required to write an end of term report on any improvements they see in their written work as well as plans for future improvements using the prescribed form. Reports are weighted at 5 per cent.
- *Entrance and Exit Writing Self-Assessment*: Students will be required to complete a self-assessment of their writing abilities and skills at the beginning and end of the module. Completed self-assessments are weighted at 5 per cent.

(Source: University of Wolverhampton course *Writing for Academic Success*. http:// www.wlv.ac.uk/shass/modules/fd1000a.html)

Wolverhampton. The criteria given to students show the kind of writing this course requires.

More detail is provided on the website (http://www.wlv.ac.uk/shass/modules/fd1000a.html) on what is expected for each type of writing the students will complete (essay, report, journal entry) and on which aspects of student drafts will be assessed and how.

THE WORDING OF ASSIGNMENTS

In this section we focus more closely on the specific forms of wording or phrasing used in assessment, for example, in assignment questions and in any guidance given to students. Students are often advised to examine assignment questions carefully to identify exactly what is required. This may be reinforced by assessment criteria or advice to students emphasising that they should address the question itself (rather than, for instance, writing down everything they know about a topic). Students may be particularly advised to look out for key words – commonly-used terms such as *describe, discuss, analyse, evaluate* – that indicate how students should approach a piece of writing. The meanings of such terms, however, are far from transparent, and may not be shared between students and lecturers (or between lecturers).

It may be worth looking over the last few assignments you have set, and identifying any key terms you have used. What meanings do they have for you? Do you tend to make a distinction between terms such as *discuss* and *evaluate*?

Figure 4.9 provides a list of meanings attributed to common assessment words. How consistent are these with your own use of such terms? You may be able to use a similar or adapted list to review the meaning of terms with your students.

Figure 4.9   Common assignment key words

- *Account for/give an account of* – 'account for' means explain, while 'give an account of' asks you to describe and analyse a series of events
- *Analyse* – separate a question or idea into its parts and discuss their relationship
- *Apply* – use concepts, theories, or methods to consider a particular case, piece of data, problem or issue
- *Assess* – evaluate or estimate the importance of something
- *Compare* – look for similarities and differences and perhaps reach a conclusion about which is preferable
- *Contrast* – set in opposition in order to bring out differences
- *Criticise/critique*– give your judgement about the merit of theories and opinions, or about the truth of facts; support your judgement with a discussion of evidence or of the reasoning involved
- *Define* – set down the precise meaning of a word or phrase; in some cases, examine different possible or often-used definitions
- *Describe* – give a detailed or graphic account
- *Discuss* – investigate or examine by argument; sift and debate; give reasons for and against
- *Evaluate* – make an appraisal of the worth of something
- *Examine* – look at something closely, questioning and exploring it
- *Explain* – make plain; interpret and account for; give reasons
- *Explore* – consider causal factors, ideas, possibilities

- *Focus on* – choose a particular aspect or strand of a problem or issue to consider
- *Illustrate* – use a figure or diagram to explain or clarify, or make clear by the use of concrete examples
- *Interpret* – expound the meaning of; make clear and explicit, usually also giving your judgement
- *Justify or prove* – build a case for an idea or perspective; use supporting evidence or logical reasoning
- *Outline* – briefly discuss or sketch the main issues or arguments about a topic
- *Report on* – give an account of a series of events that have already occurred, usually with little judgement or evaluation
- *State* – provide the main points about a topic
- *Summarise* – briefly put into your own words the main points from someone else's text

(adapted from Allen [undated] in Drew and Bingham (1997: 57))

In addition to the key words mentioned above, other aspects of assignment wording such as initial question words ('*What (is)* ...?', '*How (may)* ...?', '*To what extent* ...?') affect how assignments may be interpreted. Again, the meanings of such terms are not transparent. For instance, a question that asks 'What is the evidence for ...?' *may* simply require an account of different forms of evidence, but it is equally possible that students will be expected to evaluate the evidence and reach a conclusion about the proposition.

Given your own teaching context, how might you ensure the meaning of assignments and any guidance provided is clear (or as clear as possible) to students?

Figure 4.10 illustrates problems students may experience with question wording. It suggests that the meaning of assessment terms is not self-evident and that the meaning of a question does not reside simply in the words used. Such problems in the interpretation of assessment wording may be exacerbated in the case of non-traditional students; students with English as a second or additional language; students with experiences of different academic writing or assessment conventions – e.g. students on modular programmes; or international students (in this last case see e.g. Mayor and Swann, 2001).

Points that we would emphasise include:

- the need for continuing discussion between students and lecturers to try to ensure that existing assessment requirements are understood
- the need for discussion between lecturers on related courses to ensure that language is used consistently (or, where not, that this can be explained to students)
- the possibility of adapting assessment requirements to make these more meaningful to students.

While the emphasis so far has been on discussion and explanation (so that assessment tasks devised and evaluated by lecturers are made clear to students) it's also possible to include students in the process of assessment on more equal terms.

Figure 4.10 A problem with question wording

A student studying language and media tackled the following essay question:

Using Markman's paper 'Time, space and television commentary' as a starting point, discuss the extent to which new communications media are influencing the form and functions of modern English.

In response to this question the student produced an essay with two distinct halves. In effect, these were two 'mini-essays', one giving an account of a particular paper and the other discussing further research on English and new communications media. The student said he had done this because the question had not asked him to *relate* his discussion of the reading to other research. A similar essay question on the same course specified the need to relate the two parts. What was not made explicit in the question above was that an essay, at least in this course, was regarded as a single piece of writing in which links were expected between different parts (e.g. a later part might build on, or extend, arguments made in an earlier part).

STUDENTS' PARTICIPATION IN ASSESSMENT

In this section we consider different ways in which students may contribute to assessment, collaborating with each other or with lecturers in assessing their own or others' writing. Reynolds and Trehan refer to this as 'participative assessment', which they characterise as: 'a process in which students and tutors share, to some degree, the responsibility for making evaluations and judgements about students' written work, gaining insights into how such judgements are made and finding appropriate ways to communicate them' (2000: 270). Participative assessment may involve *self-assessment*, where students make an evaluation of their own work; *peer assessment*, where students evaluate the work of other students; or some combination of the two.

Examples of self-assessment

Self-assessment is often designed to encourage students to take greater responsibility for their own learning. At a minimal level it might involve students submitting a comment on their assignment – noting, for instance, what they think they have done well, and how their writing could be improved. The lecturer could then take account of these comments in marking the assignment. Students may also participate more fully in the assessment process. They could, for example, negotiate a piece of writing with a lecturer and perhaps also criteria for assessment. The student's own evaluation of their writing could be submitted with the assignment, and a grade negotiated with the lecturer.

Do you already use any form of self- or peer assessment? If not, could this have anything to offer within your own teaching context?

Examples of peer assessment

There is a wide range of assessment practices which involve some form of student participation in the assessment of other students. For instance, students might provide comments on the work of other students, using a set of agreed criteria. Students might also grade the work of other students, with grades moderated by the lecturer. Some forms of peer assessment minimise the involvement of the lecturer – for instance, students' completion of an assignment, and its assessment by other students, may be recorded but the lecturer may not read the assignment.

Students' participation may also be less formal: the process of peer review discussed in Chapter 2, in which students comment on drafts of one another's work, could be considered a type of formative assessment. Students might also give a seminar presentation that is commented on by other students and then written up as a paper for summative assessment by a lecturer.

Participating in assessment may give students greater insights into, and understanding of the assessment process itself, and also the kinds of writing that are valued within a particular discipline. It provides student writers with a wider range of judgements about their writing. Where students are involved in decision-making about assessment, in principle this may become less hierarchical and more democratic. In some cases – such as professionally-oriented courses – students' participation in assessment is consistent with processes that they are engaged in in their professional lives (i.e. evaluating the work of others in various ways). More pragmatically, in cases where peer assessment reduces lecturers' involvement, it saves lecturers marking time.

If you regard students' participation in assessment as important you may wish to assess some aspect of the participation process itself. For one example of this, see Figure 4.11.

Figure 4.11 Taking account of peer comments in assessment

In a course in which students routinely received comments from other students on a first draft of their work, they were asked to submit these comments with their final piece of writing for assessment. They were also asked to indicate how they had taken account of comments in producing their final version. This process was designed to assess students' responsiveness to comments, and their ability to improve their work, as well as the final product.

Further considerations

There are several potential benefits to participative forms of assessment (as suggested above), but there are also certain dangers. Reynolds and Trehan comment that, although at least some forms of participative assessment seem less hierarchical than more traditional 'lecturer-dominated' assessment, institutional hierarchies are rarely challenged. At a local level, students may defer to the judgement of lecturers. More generally, assessment must satisfy a number of institutional constraints, which in practice limits what students can do. As in other forms of assessment, power is also an issue. Downplaying one source of power (the lecturer) doesn't mean that relations between participants become equal. For instance, students on a management course in which assignments were evaluated by a small group of fellow-students mentioned certain reservations about the outcomes of this process:

The whole assessment process relies on us to be open ... both in giving and taking comments, including criticism ... but often this was not the case ... Instead what really happens is that people sort things out informally ... groups of individuals always working together with other groups ... struggles for power ... different people having their own agendas.

You can present what's expected ... [by the other students] ... that way you're always guaranteed a good mark. Looking back it's easy to see how powerful individuals got what they wanted.

(Reynolds and Trehan, 2000: 274)

For those committed to more participative forms of assessment there is a need first to understand the processes (from institutional to interpersonal) that may militate against this and then to confront these explicitly with students.

Students will also need some form of training in marking an assessment – they could, for instance, carry out a marking exercise as a group. It may be useful to provide a checklist for students to use when assessing their own and others' work, as in the self-assessment checklist in Figure 4.12.

You may prefer to negotiate a checklist with students. However, any checklist needs to be tied in to assessment criteria and at least discussed with students to ensure assessment requirements are shared by all participants.

PRE-EMPTING PLAGIARISM

Plagiarism, or even the suspicion of it, can have serious consequences for students. Universities frequently publish policy statements on plagiarism, but these often highlight the severity of punishment, rather than providing students with guidance on how to avoid it. Understanding that plagiarism is wrong is not sufficient for students, nor does it help lecturers reinforce good practice in student writing. Students are often unsure of the conventions for citing the work of others and how to successfully integrate quotations, ideas and concepts as supporting evidence for arguments. Fear of being suspected of 'cheating' may lead to over-referencing, where essays don't display a confident grasp of the subject. A research project looked into the views of lecturers on this issue, and why they thought plagiarism occurred (Goodman, 2002). While

Figure 4.12 Checklist for students to use as part of self-assessment

Covering information
My title/cover page shows clearly:
My name
Course title and number
Tutor's name
The question I have chosen
Date assignment handed in

Introduction
The introduction:
Sets the question topic against a wider background
Clarifies my understanding of the question/topic
Defines key or problematic terms
Outlines the approach I will be taking to the question/topic

Main text
In the main body of the assignment:
My key points are clearly presented
The points I make are systematically backed up by facts/evidence/examples/
arguments
Quotations and references to other works are accurately cited
Any diagrams, figures or tables are labelled properly

Conclusions
The conclusion:
Brings together the main points
Links back to the question/topic
States clearly my conclusion(s)

Style and presentation
Overall, the assignment:
Reads clearly throughout
Makes correct use of spelling, grammar and punctuation
Accurately lists the background reading I have consulted
Is within the word limits specified

(Hounsell, 1995; cited in Brown *et al.*, 1997: 71)

a few respondents said that they thought some students cheated for reasons of expediency or lack of interest in the subject, the vast majority saw plagiarism as an academic writing difficulty. Students struggled to understand how to use sources and reference them appropriately, or they lacked confidence in their writing ability or felt they had nothing worthwhile of their own to say. This view is a far cry from one of the current 'moral panics' engendered by increasing use of the Internet, where students are suspected of downloading and submitting essays on a regular basis, although this does occur and is discussed in Chapter 6.

Many teachers have learned to identify – and avoid – plagiarism through osmosis, we 'know it when we see it', but few of us think it through until confronted with something that seems eerily familiar. Pennycook (1996) questions the wisdom of expecting original work from students, partly because all language is recycled from different contexts, and partly because academia itself is full of re-use of others' work and ideas which are not always attributed. That said, students need to develop confidence in incorporating sources into their writing and referencing them appropriately.

What sort of guidance do you (or your institution) provide for students about plagiarism? How detailed is it, and how could it be improved?

There are a number of ways in which plagiarism can be approached with students. Some suggestions are provided here.

- Deal explicitly with the issue. Few students seem to feel that plagiarism has been clearly explained. Most institutions have some policy on plagiarism, but this may not take account of the fact that not all students 'cheat' deliberately. Make it clear what is an acceptable citation and what is not. The advice you give will reflect your discipline area and its conventions, and your views on what is acceptable in students' writing.
- Look at available institutional guidance and identify areas which are not covered in sufficient detail for your purposes. You could provide something like Figure 4.13.
- Consider spending some time in a session with your students using paraphrases as an exercise to draw up collective ground rules for your group. There are some excellent websites on this topic, which provide examples of acceptable and unacceptable paraphrasing, with reasons, and strategies for avoiding inadvertent plagiarism. For example, see Figure 4.14.
- If you feel a deeper level of linguistic detail is useful for your students, you could show them examples of clumsy paraphrases which would probably be considered plagiarism. An example is shown in Figure 4.15.

Figure 4.13 How to avoid accidental plagiarism

Expect to acknowledge everything you've got from a source other than your own head. The things that don't need referencing are your own ideas and common or uncontroversial knowledge (*English is a Germanic language*, for example). If in doubt, err on the side of *over*-referencing, until you get the knack. Having too many references in a text breaks up the flow of your writing, but that is the lesser of two evils. To avoid too much repetition, you may be able to say at the beginning of a section or paragraph: *The following is a summary of information given in Smith (1994)*. Note, however, that it is *not* sufficient to give one vague reference to your source somewhere, and then draw directly from it page after page.

(Wray et al., 1998: 242)

Figure 4.14   How to recognise unacceptable and acceptable paraphrases

How to recognise unacceptable and acceptable paraphrases

Here's the original text, from page 1 of *Lizzie Borden: A Case Book of Family and Crime in the 1890s* by Joyce Williams et al.:

The rise of industry, the growth of cities, and the expansion of the population were the three great developments of late nineteenth-century American history. As new, larger, steam-powered factories became a feature of the American landscape in the East, they transformed farm hands into industrial laborers, and provided jobs for a rising tide of immigrants. With industry came urbanization the growth of large cities (like Fall River, Massachusetts, where the Bordens lived) which became the centers of production as well as of commerce and trade.

Here's an unacceptable paraphrase that is plagiarism:

The increase of industry, the growth of cities, and the explosion of the population were three large factors of nineteenth-century America. As steam-driven companies became more visible in the eastern part of the country, they changed farm hands into factory workers and provided jobs for the large wave of immigrants. With industry came the growth of large cities like Fall River where the Bordens lived which turned into centers of commerce and trade as well as production.

What makes this passage plagiarism?

The preceding passage is considered plagiarism for two reasons:

* the writer has only changed around a few words and phrases, or changed the order of the original's sentences.
* the writer has failed to cite a source for any of the ideas or facts.

If you do either or both of these things, you are plagiarising.

   Note: This paragraph is also problematic because it changes the sense of several sentences (for example, 'steam-driven companies' in sentence two misses the original's emphasis on factories). Here's an acceptable paraphrase:

Fall River, where the Borden family lived, was typical of northeastern industrial cities of the nineteenth century. Steam-powered production had shifted labor from agriculture to manufacturing, and as immigrants arrived in the US, they found work in these new factories. As a result, populations grew, and large urban areas arose. Fall River was one of these manufacturing and commercial centers (Williams 1).

Why is this passage acceptable?

This is acceptable paraphrasing because the writer:

* accurately relays the information in the original
* uses her own words
* lets her reader know the source of her information.

(University of Indiana at Bloomington.
http://www.indiana.edu/~wts/wts/plagiarism.html#original)

Referencing conventions may differ in different countries and educational systems, so it is worth talking through with students what their expectations are. For students from different cultures, it will be interesting to hear how academic writing practices in their context may differ. A Chinese student in Buranen's research, for example, said that listing all your sources in a bibliography could be seen as 'an insult to the reader's intelligence' as readers were expected to know the source (Buranen, 1999). A group exercise with exemplification, as shown in Figures 4.14 and 4.15, and discussion may be the most productive way of raising the students' confidence on this issue.

Figure 4.15 Plagiarism resulting from clumsy paraphrasing

Source

Attempting (verb) to find the causes and effects of social relations among people, sociology (noun), a part of the science (noun) of human behaviour, studies (verb) the intercommunication and interaction among persons and groups.

Paraphrase

In an attempt (noun) to find the causes and effects of social relations among people, a sociologist (new noun), who is a scientist (new noun) of human behaviour, undertakes studies (noun) of the intercommunication and interaction among persons and groups.

(Clough, 2000. http://www.dcs.shef.ac.uk/~cloughie/plagiarism/HTML_Version/)

CONCLUSION

This chapter has discussed a range of strategies for the assessment of student writing, while conceding that there is no 'ideal' form of assessment – it is necessarily constrained by institutional and other factors. We have also emphasised that a key issue in assessment is the need to ensure that students understand fully what you are looking for in evaluating their writing. We began with the example of a law student who was confused by the use of certain terms (such as *argue*) and who was also unclear about the audience for her writing. In this case, clearer guidance and time spent unravelling the lecturer's expectations might have helped her feel more confident about her work.

As British higher education moves towards the practice of more explicit criteria being communicated to students, it's worth returning to the first principles of some traditional expectations and considering whether they serve their intended purposes. For example, distributing lists of essay questions may not be the best (and is certainly not the only) way of assessing students' learning. This chapter has outlined some alternatives and highlighted the need to reflect upon what students need to know to complete particular assignments, and what the best way of assessing this knowledge might be. We have also considered the extent to which students may be involved more fully in the assessment process – for instance in the development of suitable forms of assessment, or in contributing to the evaluation of their own or others' work. Chapter 5 continues some of this discussion, focusing particularly on the purposes and nature of feedback given to students on their writing.

NOTE

1   Lillis, 1999: 135–8.

Chapter 5

Giving feedback on student writing

Making sense of feedback[1]

Feedback on student's essay
The discussion of poverty and the disagreements surrounding its definition are well made but for this essay needed to be reduced down to what you feel is the most relevant aspect of this discussion.

Student comment on feedback
How do you know which bits are worth defining and which bits aren't? Cause for me, everything is new and I think, well maybe, you know, she's *(tutor)* looking for this. Or maybe this is more important to her, I mean I don't know, I can't pinpoint things.

INTRODUCTION

The feedback given here on a first-year undergraduate course in sociology is typical of much written feedback to be found on students' texts, containing three elements which many lecturers would consider to be useful: a positive comment, *well made*; a criticism, *needed to be reduced down*; and a suggestion for improvement, *what you feel is the most relevant*. However, the usefulness of such feedback is put into question by the student's response. First, the student doesn't pick up on the lecturer's positive comment but only the negative, so she does not seem to recognise what it is that she has done well. Second, she doesn't know how to make sense of the more critical suggestion that she focus on what is relevant: as the student says, being told to select what she feels to be most relevant seems a strange demand because how do you know which bits are worth defining? Thus whilst the lecturer has clearly aimed to offer a thoughtful commentary on the student's text, the overall experience of the student writer turns out to be one of frustration.

The above extracts foreground for us fundamental questions which must be addressed in thinking about our daily practice of commenting on student writing: what is good feedback? And how can we communicate our comments in ways which are meaningful to students? This chapter aims to explore these questions by focusing on:

- current institutional demands for feedback and insights from research
- the purposes and focus of feedback
- commentary on students' texts
- ways of communicating feedback to students
- the development of 'feedback dialogues'.

The focus of this chapter is mainly on lecturers (subject specialists) and tutors (writing and study support staff) commenting on students' writing. The role of students in responding to one another's writing was discussed in Chapter 2 (peer review) and Chapter 4 (peer assessment). However, many of the points we make will be relevant to anyone commenting on writing. Where points apply particularly to subject specialists, writing tutors or students we indicate this.

The evidence we have about feedback comes largely from feedback given in written form, but many of the general principles discussed in this chapter would apply also to spoken or electronic feedback. Where any points we make relate just to one type of feedback (e.g. spoken or written), again, we indicate this.

INSTITUTIONAL DEMANDS AND RESEARCH INSIGHTS

The provision of feedback on students' writing is a central pedagogic practice in higher education. Much feedback takes the form of comments produced as part of assessment. Such feedback practices have come under scrutiny in many contexts. In the UK, for instance, the Quality Assurance Agency (QAA), the national body that reviews academic standards and the quality of teaching and learning in higher education, outlined the following principles which should govern the provision of feedback to students. While these are expressed at institutional level, they are clearly targeted at the practices of individual lecturers:

> Institutions should ensure that appropriate feedback is provided to students on assessed work in a way that promotes learning and facilitates improvement. In meeting the needs of students for feedback on their progress and attainment, institutions will need to consider:

- the timeliness of feedback
- specifying the nature and extent of feedback that students can expect in relation to particular types and units of assessment, and whether this is to be accompanied by the return of assessed work
- the effective use of comments on returned work, including relating feedback to assessment criteria, in order to help students identify areas for improvement as well as commending them for evident achievement
- the role of oral feedback, either on a group or individual basis as a means of supplementing written feedback
- when feedback may not be appropriate.

(Quality Assurance Agency, 2000)

Research on feedback suggests that it is a complex process (perhaps more complex than is implied by the QAA principles). The following emerge as points of broad consensus from a range of research studies:

- the purposes of feedback are often mixed and left unstated
- there is often a mismatch between lecturers' and students' understanding about what is required in academic writing
- students may find lecturers' comments unclear, confusing, vague
- students may meet with different (and inconsistent) comments from different lecturers on similar pieces of writing
- the kinds of feedback lecturers provide, and the way this is expressed, are informed by lecturers' disciplinary backgrounds, personal interests and values
- feedback does not always correspond to published guidelines or criteria
- feedback is often not as helpful as either lecturers or students would like it to be
- giving and receiving feedback is an emotional, as well as a rational activity.[2]

There are also continuing debates both within research and amongst lecturers over important questions such as: what kind of feedback is most valuable to students? Which is more/less useful – spoken or written feedback? Do students make use of feedback comments or are they primarily interested in the grade? How can lecturers most effectively word their comments to students?

This chapter attempts to work from the points of consensus whilst acknowledging that there are many things we still don't know about the nature of feedback and how it is understood by lecturers and students. Our aim is to help you think about ways in which you might more effectively construct feedback in line with your concerns and priorities. Depending on whether you are a subject lecturer or a writing tutor you may decide that particular areas of feedback are your responsibility. Exactly what you decide you should be commenting on will obviously depend on your area of expertise and your role in developing students' writing.

IDENTIFYING THE PURPOSES OF FEEDBACK

As a starting point it may be worth considering the purposes for which you usually respond to students' writing, and making an inventory of your own feedback practices. The list below suggests some examples.

Purposes for providing feedback might include:

- to support students' writing development
- to teach, or reinforce, a particular aspect of disciplinary content
- to teach specific academic writing conventions
- to indicate strengths and weaknesses of a piece of writing (perhaps in relation to a set of criteria)
- to explain or justify a grade
- to suggest how a student may improve in their next piece of writing.

We suggested in Chapter 4 that a distinction is commonly made between summative assessment, which is designed formally to evaluate a student's performance, and formative assessment, which is designed to support a student's learning. But we also noted that, in practice, these functions were often combined. Different purposes for feedback, similarly, are frequently combined – feedback may be intended, for instance, both to justify a grade and to teach students.

Having thought about your purposes in giving feedback, it is important to consider your actual feedback practices – i.e. what aspects of students' writing you actually comment on in giving feedback to students. In the next section we focus on some examples of tutor feedback comments, point to the difficulties involved in making meaningful comments on students' writing and suggest some ways in which comments can be of more use to students.

COMMENTING ON STUDENTS' WRITING

Consider again the example of feedback and the student's response at the beginning of this chapter. A key point about this example is that the feedback seems to be, and indeed to a certain extent is, about the *content* of the writing: the sociology lecturer is concerned with commenting on the student writer's understanding and treatment of poverty in the essay, which is a key area of this particular university course. However, whilst an interest in content drives much tutor feedback, it is important to recognise that comments on content are often (if not always) embedded in concerns about academic writing conventions and it is these conventions which are often so problematic for student writers.

Activity 5.1 Giving feedback

Jot down what you feel it is important to comment on in students' writing. When you have done this, compare your list with your actual feedback practices – perhaps by checking through a small sample of marked assignments. The areas you have commented on might include some of those listed in the left hand column.

spelling grammatical accuracy	linguistic accuracy
introduction conclusion overview of literature	text structure
getting referencing conventions right use of specialist terminology use of formal or informal language	register
appropriate forms of argument reference to literature/ other appropriate sources use of personal experience a critical perspective	rhetorical purpose
relevance to question factual errors	content
other?	

Have you commented on some things more/less than you would have expected? Does the balance between the different aspects of feedback that you give (e.g. content, text structure, linguistic accuracy) seem appropriate? Are there certain things that you downplay or ignore? It may be, for instance, that you focus on aspects of writing that are readily specifiable and relatively straightforward to correct (e.g. spelling errors, referencing conventions); or that you are cautious about identifying too many errors for fear of discouraging students. Are there things that you have written that you are surprised about/dissatisfied with? How closely do you think your purposes in giving feedback are reflected in what you actually do?

Given the confusion that surrounds students' understanding of feedback, it is important to be as clear as possible about the rationale and focus of your comments. This is particularly the case when more than one person is involved in commenting on and assessing students' texts. In this latter context, it would be helpful to students if different roles and aims were distinguished – i.e. to identify who will focus on what. If you wish to use some form of peer review (see Chapter 2), again it is important to discuss with students what their comments focus on, and how these will differ from any comments that you provide.

It may be that you are satisfied with the focus of your comments but would like to provide more explicit feedback on specific aspects of the students' texts. Ideas for more explicit commentary relating to the framework we have discussed in the book – linguistic accuracy, text structure, register, rhetorical purpose – can be found in Chapters 2 and 3. In Activity 5.2 we illustrate why students find it difficult to make sense of some lecturer and tutor feedback and why more specific and detailed commentary may be needed.

The statement 'faulty grammar' in Activity 5.2 does not help the student in this instance to understand what was wrong with this bit of her text. In fact, it is not clear what 'faulty grammar' refers to. One feature which could be identified as 'faulty' is the use of 'who' instead of 'that' after 'element'. We assume however that by 'faulty grammar' the lecturer is referring to the sequence 'power struggle between individuals or groups within a society or between nation states' – a clause in which there is no finite (main) verb. Where possible, students need to be told explicitly where and how their 'grammar' is incorrect; this may be easier

Activity 5.2 Making sense of feedback

Consider the extract below from a student's writing for a sociology course, and the lecturer's written comment. Where do you think the 'faulty grammar' is in the student's extract?

Extract from student's text	Lecturer's comment written alongside this section but with no specific part of the text marked
The conflict model of society is based on social order that is not agreed. There is some element of stability by one element who impose order, power struggle between individuals or groups within a society or between nation states.	FAULTY GRAMMAR

to organise where subject lecturers are working in partnership with writing/study skills/EAP tutors who are used to focusing on linguistic aspects of writing. Where the subject lecturer is unsure about how to explain grammatical errors, providing an alternative sentence or sentences can be useful. In this instance, the student could be given alternatives such as 'There is a power struggle between individuals or groups within a society or between nation states'; or 'A conflict model of society assumes that there is …'.

As we discussed in Chapter 2, it is important to help students identify errors in their own writing. It is also important to consider why such errors may be being made. The list in Figure 5.1 gives some examples. You may be able to use such a list in giving feedback to students, or encourage them to construct their own lists and use these in future writing. Of course, it is important to indicate that there is often debate over what constitutes an 'error' in grammar. Consider example 3 in Figure 5.1. Would you be happy to accept the student's version in this case? Activity 5.3 explores these issues.

Figure 5.1 Some common errors in student writing[3]

Some common problems	What's going on?	Possible feedback comment
1 *'Clumsy sentences'* Example from student's text: *If in the software industry things get patched up and without social responsibilities in the event such patching up could lead to damage it would be ignored.*	Writer trying to formulate and express idea which involves several strands.	• Suggest breaking into two sentences. • Offer alternative sentence(s) such as: *A job which is badly carried out in the software industry might lead to damage. If a software engineer has no sense of social responsibility, such damage could go unnoticed.* • Check out with writer what exactly she is trying to say: *What do you mean here? Can you think of another way of writing this?*
2 *'Not a complete sentence'* Example: *Leaving many questions unanswered.*	Writer may be influenced by spoken language patterns where boundaries between grammatical units are marked differently (through intonation and pausing, for example).	• Introduce some 'metalanguage' such as *subject* and *finite* or *main verb* and *clause*. Give examples of simple and more complex clauses. • Simple sentence with one clause = *There are many questions left unanswered.* Complex sentence with two clauses = *There are many questions left unanswered so it is important to reconsider the methodology.*

continued ...

Figure 5.1 continued

3 *'Where's the full stop?'* Example: *These two have a common focus, both stress the systemic nature of society.*	Writer is making decisions about the use of commas/full stops on the basis of pauses in spoken language rather than on the structure of written language.	• Ask writer why she is using a comma here. • Introduce some metalanguage/ specialist terminology such as subject and finite or main verb and clause, and explain that full stops need to be based on clause structure rather than on 'sound', such as listening out for pauses.
4 *'These sentences don't make sense'* Example: *In fact all types of West Indian Creoles should be viewed along a continuum. However, there is a large number of Creole speakers, but no one uses a creolised speech to the same extent.*	Mistaken use of conjunction. *However* signals a departure from the previous idea, whereas in fact, the second sentence seems to be reinforcing the idea expressed in the first sentence. Writer not aware that 'linking words' carry specific meanings.	• Check out what the writer is trying to say and offer alternative conjunction. • Possible alternative conjunction or signposting here would be, 'Indeed...' (see Chapter 2).

Feedback comments on register in terms of formality are also problematic for students, partly because tutors and lecturers have a range of views on academic register. Activity 5.3 explores these issues.

Activity 5.3 Formal and informal language in academic writing

A starting point for making explicit your view on register with student writers is to discuss specific linguistic features that you accept or reject. You can discuss this in terms of formality, as illustrated below.

What is your view on the use of the following?

Contracted or full verb forms?	I'm, she's, they can't	I am, she is, they cannot
Colloquial or more formal expressions?	She slagged him off	In a derogatory way
Non-standard or standard forms?	She were, they was	She was, they were
'Everyday' or subject specific terms	Changing from one language to another	Code-switching
The use or not of the first-person, 'I'	I think there are three main reasons why it is important to explore the value of talk in learning.	There are three main reasons why it is important to explore the value of talk in learning.

Different lecturers accept different uses of language but students certainly need to be told about your expectations and preferences. It may be that you will accept or expect greater or lesser levels of formality according to how long students have been writing in your discipline. You may accept different levels of formality according to the text type they are being asked to produce: for journal writing informal language may be preferred above the more formal writing usually associated with academic essays. Students need to know about your views.

It is also important to encourage students to see that decisions around language use are not necessarily straightforward. For example, whilst the use of the first-person (*I, we*) is often discouraged in academic writing, in practice it is used in different ways and for different purposes. Activity 5.4 explores these uses.

Activity 5.4 Some uses of first-person forms in academic writing

The examples set out some ways in which first-person forms (*I, we, us*) may be used in academic writing. How might you use these examples, or similar examples from your own subject area, to discuss with students your own and their views about different uses of the first-person?

*   *'I'/'We' as the representative*
    Example: The differentiation of British and American English causes us to ponder about the right form of Standard English.

*   *'I'/'We' as the guide*
    Example: So far we have said nothing about the 'sense' of words.

*   *'I' as the architect*
    Example: I will concentrate on the period of the Renaissance.

*   *'I' as the recounter of the research process*
    Example: I tape recorded a conversation with each co-researcher.

*   *'I'/'We' as the opinion-holder*
    Example: Looking back at Kushwant Singh's words, we can determine from this period that English did indeed absorb the languages it came into contact with.

(Tang and John, 1999: Appendix)

It may be that you want students to avoid the first-person altogether, or to reduce their use of this considerably. It would help students if you could suggest ways of doing this whilst still constructing an argument (see Chapters 2 and 3).

WAYS OF COMMUNICATING FEEDBACK

In this section we switch from a focus on the specific content of feedback – *what* lecturers choose to comment on in students' writing – to look at *how* feedback on students' work may be communicated. Particular ways of communicating feedback contribute to what may be said (or what may be said most easily); to students' understanding of the comments they receive; to what they feel about these comments; and to the establishment of a particular kind of relationship between lecturer and student, or, more generally, those who give and receive feedback. We consider first individual and group feedback; then the possibilities afforded by spoken as compared with written feedback; what we have termed 'feedback formats' – the extent to which written feedback is structured or open-ended; the kinds of language used in feedback; and finally the 'look' of feedback – where and how this is presented to students.

Individual and group feedback

While a great deal of feedback responds to the work of individual students, many lecturers also include an element of group feedback. Guidance sheets on 'common errors', for instance, may be produced as a resource for a group of students. In responding to particular assignments, a set of general comments may be given to the whole group with individual feedback focusing on issues that are specific to a particular student's work.

Including an element of group feedback may save time by avoiding repetition of similar points in individual feedback; group discussion may also allow students to raise issues there would be little time to consider on an individual basis; and students may be reassured by seeing that others have had similar problems. However, because the lecturer's comments will tend to be expressed at a general level, students may not always be able to relate these to their own writing (or their own concerns).

The use of spoken feedback

Although the research evidence cited in this chapter derives mainly from written feedback, many of the points we have made would also apply to face-to-face discussion. However, discussion also facilitates certain kinds of feedback: while (potentially) time-consuming, it may also be revealing, giving you a fuller understanding of what a student is trying to achieve in their writing, or of sources of errors. Figure 5.2 provides an example of individualised spoken feedback. In this case, the student had misused the conjunction 'however' (the example comes from Figure 5.1 above). Discussion with the student revealed that, while she had been using 'however' in a structurally appropriate way, she had misunderstood the meaning of the term.

Electronic feedback falls somewhere between speech and writing. It is a written medium but is often associated with relative informality and allows more scope for discussion/negotiation. (See Chapter 6 for further discussion of the possibilities offered by electronic communication.)

Figure 5.2 Spoken feedback

Student's written text

In fact all types of West Indian Creoles should be viewed along a continuum. However, there is a large number of Creole speakers, but no one uses a creolised speech to the same extent.

Tutor's written comment

I don't understand what you're saying here.

Spoken feedback

T: Why have you used 'however'?

M: I thought, I'm starting a new sentence. If I like, go straight, say 'there' straight away, to me it doesn't sound right. ...

M: I thought 'however' meant another change of thought.

T: It does, but it means a change of direction of thought.

M: I thought it meant the same direction. Oh, a completely different idea?

T: It's like, say, I like shopping however I'm not going today.

M: Whereas I've been saying, I like going shopping however I'm going to buy some ...

(T = lecturer; M = student)

(Lillis, 2001: 154)

Feedback formats

A key issue in providing written feedback on students' work is the extent to which feedback should be structured, as opposed to entirely open-ended. We mentioned earlier that feedback sometimes depends on a lecturer's tacit understanding of what makes a good piece of writing; that students may find different lecturers orienting to different value systems which are not made explicit; and that even where published guidance or assessment criteria are available to students comments are not necessarily related to these. Using proformas that structure feedback is one way of responding to such concerns: proforma headings matching assessment criteria allow students to see what is valued in a piece of writing, and ensure that lecturers direct feedback towards agreed and explicit criteria.

Figure 5.3 shows a highly structured feedback proforma used in a social sciences course. In this case, the assessment criteria are listed in the left-hand column and the marker ticks a series of boxes to show how well students have satisfied each of these criteria. This may be contrasted with more open-ended feedback – see Figure 5.4.

Figure 5.3 Feedback proforma (Sheffield Hallam University, cited in Garner and Lillis, forthcoming)

Feedback proforma

Although the exact ways in which the proforma is used with students varies, the three boxed sets of comments are intended to indicate whether the essay is 'good' or 'poor', reading from left to right.

Introduction	provides clear outline of essay / issues	partial attempt to describe content of essay	no attempt to define scope of essay
	☐	☐	☐
Logical development / Structure	develops a logical argument	could be better organised, sequencing inappropriate	no theme or line of argument
	☐	☐	☐
Understanding	clear insight and understanding	competent use of written sources	descriptive and use of undigested sources
	☐	☐	☐
Relevance	all material relevant	some irrelevant material / repetition	much irrelevant material
	☐	☐	☐
Use of evidence	good use of examples and evidence	some use of evidence and examples	essay lacks much evidence to back up statements
	☐	☐	☐
Use of sources	critical use of a range of sources	main sources covered	only evidence of minimal reading
	☐	☐	☐
Analysis / critical discussion	substantial amount of analysis and critical discussion	some evidence of analysis and critical discussion	little analysis or critical discussion
	☐	☐	☐

Figure 5.4 Extract from open-ended comments on a student's essay

[Student's name] – you've drawn on a good range of examples in this essay, you've given good background information on the study of language variation, you've also adopted a (usefully) critical approach.

Your essay could be improved by targeting the question more explicitly. The question asks you how individuals vary their speech, and how this has been investigated. Much of the early part of your essay discusses studies of variation in very general terms, rather than drawing on these to address the question. I've marked, in the margin, the most relevant parts of your discussion of these studies.

…

It may be useful to consider your own feedback practices in this respect: to what extent do you adopt a more structured or open-ended approach? What do you think the strengths and limitations of different approaches would be within your own teaching context?

Figure 5.5 shows our assessment of the strengths and limitations of structured feedback proformas and open-ended comments such as those represented in Figures 5.3 and 5.4.

Figures 5.3 and 5.4 represent extremes – a proforma that restricts feedback entirely to a three-point scale for pre-specified criteria as opposed to entirely open-ended comments. There are clearly intermediate positions, such as (fewer) tick-boxes representing criteria followed by a space for open-ended comments; or the use of agreed headings for open-ended comments. It may be worth trying out different formats to identify what works best in relation to your own teaching.

The language of feedback

Many points discussed in Chapter 4 in relation to the language of assessment apply also to the language used in feedback. The ambiguity of certain key words such as *describe, discuss, evaluate*, and the way these may be used differently by different lecturers, is relevant to lecturers' use, and students' understanding of such terms in feedback. Since we have already addressed this issue in Chapter 4, we shall not repeat this discussion here. However, some implications that we identified for the wording of assessment tasks seem to generalise, with very little adaptation, to the production of feedback on students' work:

- there is a need for continuing discussion between students and lecturers to try to ensure that what lecturers are looking for in students' writing, and how this is communicated in feedback, are understood by students;
- there is a need for discussion between lecturers on related courses to ensure that feedback practices, including words and phrases used to characterise students' writing, are consistent (or where not, that any differences can be explained to students);
- there may be a need to adapt documentation (e.g. writing guidelines, feedback proformas) to make it more meaningful to students.

Figure 5.5   Strengths and limitations of structured feedback proformas and open-ended comments

	Feedback proformas	*Open-ended comments*
Strengths	Relate feedback to explicit criteria, shared between lecturers and students;	Allow more individualised response, focused specifically on this piece of writing;
	Ensure different lecturers orient towards the same criteria;	Can take into account the needs of different students;
	May contribute towards greater consistency between different lecturers or across related courses in a department;	Discursive text may feel more personal and friendly to student;
	Are quick to complete, saving time on courses with large numbers of students.	Feedback can acknowledge value of 'divergent' essays (i.e. essays that do not conform to your original expectations but that nevertheless have a number of strengths).
Limitations	Necessarily rigid – in this case, assumes a piece of writing can be placed at one of three points along a continuum from strong to weak;	May not relate explicitly to criteria;
	More difficult to target towards needs of different students;	Allow lecturers to orient towards different sets of values (or implicit criteria), which may not be clear to students;
	May feel rather impersonal;	May be vague, or hard for students to follow;
	Descriptors for writing may themselves be problematical: in this case, how students draw on material for their writing seems to be covered, in different ways, under 'understanding', 'relevance', 'use of evidence' and 'use of sources'; differences between these may turn out to be rather subtle.	Lengthy open-ended comments take longer to produce.

There are, however, additional language issues that relate more specifically to feedback. The first of these concerns how criticism of students' work is phrased, and in particular the need to balance negative with positive feedback. Since feedback is, by definition, evaluative, there is a danger that it may focus on shortcomings, and so become over-negative (see e.g. Ivanic *et al.*, 2000). Positive comments are important because students need to know what they have done well in addition to how their writing could be improved. There is also a danger that over-negative feedback may undermine students' confidence as writers.

Figure 5.6 represents an attempt to balance positive and negative feedback in open-ended comments on a student's essay. In what ways is this feedback similar to your approach? How do you feel a student might respond to such feedback?

Figure 5.6 Open-ended feedback

An extremely well-structured assignment, [student's name], which is very easy to follow and provides a generally comprehensive coverage of the key ideas and the important research studies. The division of your essay into two distinct sections is also helpful. Although there is a tendency for you to offer descriptive accounts you do make one or two useful evaluative comments in the first section.

When you move onto the research studies you go a long way towards recognising and expressing the strengths and/or weaknesses of the individual approaches. However, you did overlook some of the developments made to accommodation theory and audience design in particular as outlined [...] on pages 322–3. Other areas where further clarification or evaluation would have been useful are identified in your script.

This is a competent response to the question, [student's name], and there is growing evidence of your ability to select appropriate material and introduce critical evaluation. The material in [this part of the course] is both varied and demanding, but you have responded effectively and produced another strong essay.

    Best wishes
    [Tutor's name]

In figure 5.6, the student's response to the comments was generally favourable, although she notes that she would have liked additional detail on how to improve her work:

> I have found the comments and evaluation of the [assignments] very helpful so far. The comments make sense, they are positive and encouraging, but still identify the additional points that could have been made, or links that have been missed.

> … what I would find even more helpful is to know, more specifically, what I would need to do to improve my mark. It would be interesting to know, for example, whether it is the approach which needs to be redefined, or whether additional information is needed, or if there are other criteria which need to be met.

The way in which feedback is expressed has to do with particular conceptions of teaching and learning and of the relationship between teacher and learner. The language of feedback may be used to construct a relatively hierarchical and overtly didactic relationship in which the power differential between lecturer and student is emphasised; or a more collegial relationship in which the lecturer attempts to 'build students' sense of membership of the academic community' (Ivanic *et al.*, 2000: 61). Research on feedback has identified several features that, in combination, may encourage a relatively collegial relationship between lecturers and students. These include:

- questions that engage students in debate – e.g. 'Why do you think …?', 'What would happen if …?', 'What do you think the implications would be …?'
- mitigated comments – forms such as 'Perhaps …', 'You may like to consider …', 'A fuller explanation might help here', as opposed to 'bald' directives – 'Explain', 'Linkage'
- use of the first person ('I'd suggest here …') that acknowledges many types of feedback as the writer's opinion.

(Ivanic et al., 2000; Lea and Street, 2000)

However, as with other aspects of feedback, language use needs to take account of specific teaching aims and contexts. For example, it is important to consider which kinds of comment are most useful at particular points in writing: questions that engage students in debate (sometimes referred to as 'open' questions) may be more useful in relation to early drafting, in order to generate ideas, than to final or almost final drafts.

What forms of expression do you tend to use in your own feedback to students? How do these relate to the kind of relationship you are trying to establish with students?

It is also important to consider the cultural context of feedback. For instance, use of the mitigated forms set out above is based on politeness conventions that will be understood by writers and readers from similar linguistic and cultural backgrounds. Although power relations are played down, they are still there beneath the surface: a student who receives the comment, 'You may like to consider …' may be more comfortable with this than with a form such as 'Explain', but they know that, in practice, they do need to implement the lecturer's suggestion. Such knowledge may not be shared by all students, and may be particularly problematical when tutors and students do not share cultural and linguistic backgrounds. This can lead to miscommunication between lecturer and student, with students assuming they have a genuine choice (Mayor and Swann, 2001).

Open questions, mitigation and use of the first person may become formulaic. The important points, however, are to acknowledge that giving feedback is a communicative act that presupposes a certain kind of relationship between reader and writer; to consider how you wish to relate to students, as well as how you wish to draw them into specific forms of academic writing, and a specific academic community; and consider how far the language used in feedback seems conducive to such a process.

Where and how written feedback is presented

We turn finally to the 'look' of written feedback on the page: where feedback is located, how it is laid out, what writing implements are used. This may seem a trivial concern, or at least one that has to do primarily with practical matters (such as legibility) or expediency. But what feedback looks like will have a bearing on how it is received by students: there is a considerable difference between feedback that is written in red pen over a student's own text, and pencilled numbers in the margin linked to a set of word-processed comments on an attached sheet. These widespread practices are exemplified in Figures 5.7 and 5.8. You may be interested to know that the student who received the comments in Figure 5.7, and *scores*   *scores*

Findings supported the hypothesis that a significant negative correlation between extraversion and altruism did occur. The level of significance was p< 05 or less than a 5% chance of the results occurring randomly. *Now go on To state what these results imply —ie do They support Eysenck's Theory?*

INTRODUCTION

An investigation was carried out to determine whether there was a significant relationship between the personality dimension of extraversion – introversion and the trait of altruism. Extraversion is a type of personality that displays characteristics or traits such as outgoing, impulsive, risk taker. An introvert possesses traits such as persistence, rigidity, and shyness. Altruistic behaviour is when a person goes out of their way, regardless of inconvenience or difficulty, to help others. ~~The prediction was that introverts were more likely to be altruistic than extraverts were. This hypothesis was derived from Eysenck's theory of personality and the work of other researchers (Personality project p 4).~~ *The hypothesis goes at The end of this section*

Figure 5.7 Student text with tutor commentary

The way to make literacy learning more simple is to embed it in the meaningful context of L1. ①

Cummins also formalized the term 'CUP'. 'CUP' is the Common Underlying Proficiency. What Cummins states is that what is learnt in one language can be drawn upon in the use of a second language. He puts forward the idea that language skills are transferable. Cummins also implies that the bilingual learners' languages are interdependent.

① Can you give an example?

Figure 5.8 Student text with numbered comment

whose tutor regularly wrote all over her text, really liked this feedback. She felt that the tutor was enthusiastic and trying very hard to show her where she had got things right as well as wrong. However, it is also the case that many students prefer not to have their text written on and like to receive a list of comments on a separate sheet which are linked to specific sections of their text as in Figure 5.8.

In their review of feedback practices, Ivanic *et al.* suggest that pencilled comments are seen as relatively tentative, and open to negotiation; whereas, at the other extreme, a red pen is the 'symbol of teachers' superior knowledge and their right to make unchallengeable judgements'

(2000: 51). They suggest also that providing separate comments shows greater respect for a student than writing directly on the student's text. The evidence for such specific interpretations is limited and seems (in this case) to be largely anecdotal. It does suggest, however, that it is important to consider potential messages that may be conveyed by the position and layout of feedback – and perhaps to discuss with students what kind of feedback they would prefer to receive.

DEVELOPING 'FEEDBACK DIALOGUES'

Ways of developing dialogue

In this section we turn to the importance of developing 'feedback dialogues' with students about their writing. By 'feedback dialogues' we mean an approach to feedback which emphasises an exchange of views, comments and questions between students and tutors. These can be in spoken or written form, in face-to-face or on-line contexts. If lecturer and tutor feedback is to be useful, it is important to encourage students to see it as part of a dialogue or conversation with them about their writing. At its most basic, our emphasis on dialogue implies that if lecturers are going to give feedback, then they will want students to pay attention to it, and may need to think of ways of encouraging students to do so.

Consider the list in Figure 5.9. To what extent do you think it is useful to give students specific guidance on how to use feedback? What other guidance could you give?

Figure 5.9 Guidance to students on how to use feedback

- Read or listen to the comments made.
- Look for the positive comments and congratulate yourself.
- Discuss the comments with other students.
- If you don't understand a comment, ask the lecturer/tutor for clarification.
- If you don't understand which bit of your writing the comment refers to, ask the lecturer/tutor for clarification.
- Look for patterns in the comments. Do they focus on linguistic accuracy? Argument? Text structure?
- Keep a record of the most important comments and look at them when you do your next piece of writing.

At a more fundamental level, an attempt to develop dialogic exchange between lecturers and students is essential if the well-documented gap between lecturers' and students' understandings about what is required in academic writing is to be bridged. Consider again the example of written feedback and the student's response at the beginning of this chapter. Whilst the student's response indicates the limitations of such feedback, the lecturer's comments are not 'wrong'. Yet if these are the only comments that the student receives, they may not be useful. If, on the other hand, these comments were understood by both participants as one part of a longer discussion about the student's writing, there would be less frustration on the part of the student, and a greater chance that the comments would serve to 'scaffold' the student's learning. In order for feedback to function successfully as 'scaffolding' (see Chapter 1), whereby the lecturer guides and supports students in their writing, the lecturer's comments should not be seen as an end in themselves but rather as the beginning of a discussion or dialogue with students.

Whilst it is often easier to develop such dialogues when the lecturer is working with a small number of students over an extended period of time, dialogue can also be fostered within the context of large classes as well as in distance education.

Activity 5.5 Feedback dialogues

The sheets in Figures 5.10 and 5.11 were used with a group of 100 first-year undergraduates in a Communication Studies degree. Students were asked to comment in Sheet 1 (Figure 5.10) on any confusion they experienced whilst writing an assignment. Students were also asked to 'assess' their writing using the criteria set out in the standard feedback sheet (Figure 5.11). Could these or similar dialogue sheets be useful in your teaching context?

Many lecturers cannot spend time discussing assignments with individual students. However, using a proforma like that in Figure 5.10 enables the student to address the lecturer directly about any specific concerns and helps the lecturer, at a glance, to see where particular problems lie. When the lecturer completes the standard assessment feedback sheet, Figure 5.11, she or he can respond to specific uncertainties relating to assessment criteria that the student may have. Examples of

Figure 5.10 Sheet 1: Students comment on their writing

Sheet 1: THINKING ABOUT PROBLEMS/CONFUSION

Did/do you feel confused about any of the following while you were writing your essay? If the answer is yes to any of the questions, tick √ and say if/how you sorted out your confusion. Indicate if you're still confused.

If the answer is no, then leave blank.

Possible problem area	Tick if confused/ problem	How you sorted it out	Tutor comments
The essay question			
what does the essay question mean?			
what does the tutor want?	√	√ talked with other students	Is it clear now?
what does 'discuss' mean?			
Content and use of sources			
does my essay answer the question?			
how do I sort out what is relevant/irrelevant?			
when should I refer to 'experts'?			
how do I reference?	√	√ used numbers at end.	
when do I use direct quotes?			
what is plagiarism?			
can I bring in my personal view?			

Figure 5.10 Students comment on their writing (continued)

does what I've written show my understanding of key ideas?			
Structure			
what should be in an introduction?			
what should be in a conclusion?			
how much do I write on each section?	✓	Still not sure	
Argument			
what is 'argument'?			
how do I organise my content into an argument?	✓	My argument is not strong	
Language/wordings			
should I be using 'long'/complicated words?			
which words can I use?			
is my grammar okay?			
Punctuation			
what is standard punctuation? –am I using commas, semi-colons correctly?			
OTHER CONCERNS?			

Figure 5.11 Sheet 2: Students assess their writing

Sheet 2: **ASSESSING YOUR ESSAY USING STANDARD FEEDBACK SHEET**

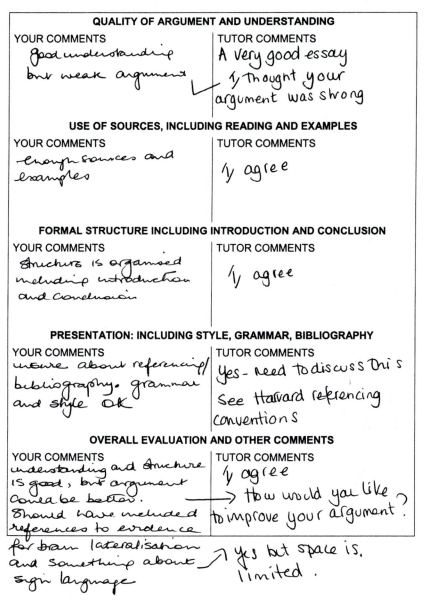

QUALITY OF ARGUMENT AND UNDERSTANDING

YOUR COMMENTS

good understanding but weak argument

TUTOR COMMENTS

A very good essay I thought your argument was strong

USE OF SOURCES, INCLUDING READING AND EXAMPLES

YOUR COMMENTS

enough sources and examples

TUTOR COMMENTS

I agree

FORMAL STRUCTURE INCLUDING INTRODUCTION AND CONCLUSION

YOUR COMMENTS

Structure is organised including introduction and conclusion

TUTOR COMMENTS

I agree

PRESENTATION: INCLUDING STYLE, GRAMMAR, BIBLIOGRAPHY

YOUR COMMENTS

unsure about referencing/ bibliography. grammar and style OK

TUTOR COMMENTS

Yes - need to discuss this See Harvard referencing conventions

OVERALL EVALUATION AND OTHER COMMENTS

YOUR COMMENTS

understanding and structure is good, but argument could be better. Should have included references to evidence for brain lateralisation and something about sign language

TUTOR COMMENTS

I agree → How would you like to improve your argument?

yes but space is limited.

such uncertainties may include questions such as, have I included enough sources? Is my argument clear? Is the essay well-structured? Have I included enough definition of key terms? Whilst answers to such questions are not straightforward, the lecturer can at least begin to respond to individual students' real concerns.

Figure 5.12 illustrates a more extended dialogue from a distance education course. Here, students were encouraged to attach an (open-ended) comment on their work when submitting an assignment. The lecturer could respond to this in their feedback on the assignment. Students were also invited, in turn, to respond to the lecturer's feedback. In this case, the initial comment was helpful in indicating a problem faced by the student: she was uncertain how legitimate it was to take issue with arguments put forward in the course materials. But the comment also had more general implications, causing the course writers to consider how far they could support students who wished to 'read against' course texts (this issue is discussed in McKinney and Swann, 2001).

Figure 5.12 Extended feedback dialogue

Student's comment on assignment

I had lots of notes, but no plan. The [assignment] had gone through four drafts, because I didn't think I could make my point clear. Also, I was not very sure whether it was appropriate to argue that Indian English, or rather its distinctive factors, are mistakes as far as I am concerned.

Extract from lecturer's feedback

[Student's name] – a good attempt at this essay. You've taken issue with the stance taken by linguists such as Verma, and constructed a counter-argument. This is fine, you don't need to agree with everything in the course and, as you say, there are linguists who take different views. In your characterisation of Indian and other 'Englishes' you are careful about detail and draw attention to several relevant aspects of the structure of English.

[…]

Student's comment on feedback received

It seems to me it's a good idea to take and support the argument of the authors of a [course book]. They clearly state their opinions and substantiate them. Arguing against them does not appear to be penalised, still, not everyone can present their argument in a favourable light. This is what might have happened in my case.

To what extent do you think similar dialogues might inform your own teaching, and the comments you make on students' writing?

Encouraging students to take responsibility

An important point about a scaffolding approach to teaching and learning writing is that whilst guidance and help are essential, the ultimate aim is to achieve what is sometimes referred to as 'handover'; that is the point at which the 'expert' tutor or lecturer hands over responsibility to the student for their own writing. Students often feel they must try to 'give tutors what they want' and to 'play it safe' and may go through the whole of their university studies without feeling that they should take responsibility for the writing that they do. Given the higher education aim of developing autonomy and critical awareness, students need to be encouraged to see that they can make choices about how they write in academia. It may be useful to discuss with students the kinds of issues they face in making choices and taking responsibility for their own writing.

Consider the extracts in Figure 5.13 from one student who wrote about her struggles around taking responsibility for her own academic writing. She was studying a course on politics and international relations. How might you use this account with students to raise questions about their responsibility as writers and the choices they face?

Figure 5.13 A student's account of taking responsibility for her writing

---

Do students see themselves merely as receivers of ideas and feel constrained about being too clever for their own good marks-wise? Or do they see themselves as people who take on the role of challenging authority, who investigate, analyze and present new ideas and their own views and thoughts?

For myself, I have to confess I used to be more of the first type, the one who likes to play it safe. It never failed to work for me. My marks might not have been outstanding, but they were good enough. You simply write a bland, uncontroversial essay and refrain from committing yourself, such as by avoiding using the pronoun 'I', and expressions like 'in my view', 'in my opinion' in your writing, and by over-attributing to sources. This latter certainly belongs to the writing convention that many students everywhere, and even today, are being taught.

[...]

I believe it is important for students to be able to argue their case and present the arguments convincingly, and to be confident enough to take and show personal responsibility for their writing.

(Don Chuan Yeoh, in Clark *et al.*, 1990: 98)

CONCLUSION

In this chapter, we have covered several aspects of feedback. We have tried both to provide examples of current practice, and to consider their strengths and limitations. We have emphasised, throughout, the importance of feedback for teaching and learning, as well as the fact that there is a strong affective dimension to giving and receiving feedback. We have also suggested that feedback will (necessarily) differ in different teaching contexts: while there is evidence that feedback is not always as effective as it might be, what counts as effective feedback will differ, to some extent, between different lecturers and students, academic areas, cultural contexts, etc. Bearing in mind this qualification, there are a number of ways in which we believe feedback may be improved. We have set these out below as a set of points to consider in relation to your own feedback practices, rather than as a set of prescriptive guidelines.

In thinking about how you can improve the feedback you provide on students' writing, we would suggest that the following points are particularly relevant:

- the timing of feedback (how often can you provide feedback, at which stages in the writing process, how soon after receiving students' writing?); clearly there are institutional and personal constraints here, but Ivanic *et al.* (2000) suggest it is worth considering whether a course may be restructured to allow time for more and better feedback
- the specific purposes you have for providing feedback – and how these will affect the nature of the feedback you provide
- what you wish to focus on in commenting on students' work (e.g. the extent to which you prioritise students' knowledge and understanding of course content and/or how effectively this is communicated; what specific writing conventions you regard as important)
- what should be the focus of different sets of comments (e.g. from a subject specialist, writing tutor, fellow students) on the same student's writing
- how far you are able to engage in discussion with lecturers on other courses taken by your students to ensure greater consistency or to manage any necessary differences in feedback practices

- what guidance you can provide for students on the kind(s) of writing you are looking for; how you can effectively relate feedback to such guidance
- what you can do to ensure feedback practices, and the specific wording of feedback are understood by students
- how you can word feedback to engage in the kind of teaching you feel is important (e.g. to provide positive comments, to question, or to engage in debate with students)
- how feedback may be used to foster a particular kind of relationship with students (e.g. the kinds of feedback that may encourage a more collegial relationship)
- where and how you write feedback (i.e. bearing in mind that the 'look' of feedback can also convey messages to students about the value set on their writing and the kind of relationship you wish to establish with them)
- whether you can adopt feedback practices that encourage greater dialogue with students (e.g. through tutorials, group discussion, written dialogues)
- how you can take account of differences between students (e.g. differences in academic, linguistic, cultural backgrounds)
- how students can be encouraged to take responsibility for their own writing.

NOTES

1 Lillis and Turner, 2001: 60–1.
2 See discussions in Chanock, 2000; Higgins, Hartley and Skelton, 2001 and 2002; Ivanic, Clark and Rimmershaw, 2000; Lea and Street, 2000; Lillis, 1999; Pardoe, 1994; Storch and Tapper, 2000; Webster, Pepper and Jenkins, 2000.
3 All examples are taken from authentic students' texts. The first example has been published in Lillis, 1996: 97; and the second in Lillis, 2001: 154.

Chapter 6

Academic writing in an electronic environment

Using technology for the first time
Sarah is a lecturer on a business studies course. Recently she has been asked to transform a traditional face-to-face business diploma into an on-line course. She has no experience of using technology to teach subject content but has heard that it can be a useful medium for enhancing student discussion and developing their academic writing.

INTRODUCTION[1]

Sarah's need to engage with technology as a teaching and learning tool is increasingly common. This chapter discusses how technology can be used in a variety of ways to facilitate students' control of academic writing. Applications can be basic (such as word-processing) or complex (such as running an entire course on-line using conferencing software). Our aims here are:

- to provide a general overview of the forms of technology which can be put to use in developing student writing
- to examine the use of Internet-based resources in developing students' writing
- to examine the use of electronic conferencing to enhance student writing
- to reflect on issues raised by the use of technology such as plagiarism.

First, we provide an overview of some of the most relevant applications of technology which can be used to develop student writing, shown diagrammatically in Figure 6.1. Then we explore in detail the contribution of electronic conferencing.

Most universities provide computing services in some form, so students who are unable to buy their own computer should now be able to access one. Technology may not radically alter what students *do* when engaged

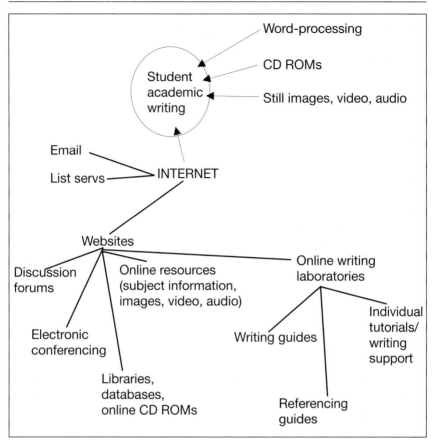

Figure 6.1 Student writing and technology: a map of resources

in the process of writing, but it does have a facilitating effect. It permits rapid transfer of information, resources and ideas among students, and exchanges between students on different campuses, or in different countries and cultures. You and your students are probably already very familiar with some uses of technology such as word-processing and electronic mail (email). Word-processing allows for extensive revision of work, and students may find the grammar, spelling and word-count tools useful. Students vary considerably in how they work, however: some students may use word-processing only for their final draft, having worked and revised on paper; whereas others write directly on screen. If you allow or ask students to revise written work in response to feedback from you or their peers, it may be helpful to require them to work on the computer so they do not have to re-type their work. Word-processors make a valuable contribution in terms of producing a tidy, legible piece of work. They may also, however, save less time than expected in that writers are often tempted to keep re-drafting.

Electronic mail allows students to contact each other and the lecturer rapidly, and to share resources and ideas. Currently email is used in at least four main ways: private communication, sending messages to conference systems (more on this below), sending assignments to lecturers, and sending and receiving messages from Listservs[2] on the Internet. Students may write more extensively and freely when using electronic media as they increasingly rely on email for both personal and academic communication. Lecturers may need to set ground rules when establishing email contact with students – some will contact their lecturer frequently and expect an immediate reply. If students need special fonts or mathematical characters in their writing, computing departments need to be alerted to see how this can be accommodated.

We turn now to writing resources which are available, or can be set up on, the Internet. You and your students may find the glossary of computer terms in Figure 6.2 useful.

Figure 6.2 Glossary of computer terms

The following list of terms can be used as a resource for students new to on-line learning and writing.

Asynchronous communication
Communication (usually via some form of information technology) between people who are distanced by time and geography. The communication is not usually instantaneous. For example, an individual in London could leave a message in the evening for an individual in Australia, who might reply to the message in their evening (i.e. ten hours later).

Computer conferencing
Computer conferencing is communication in which groups of people can communicate electronically. The software involved enables the creation of 'spaces' where participants can leave and read messages.

Computer mediated communication (CMC)
Communication between individuals and groups using any form of information technology (e.g. email or a computer conferencing system).

Computer supported collaborative work
Collaborative group work carried out through computer mediated communication, rather than by the group meeting in person or talking over the telephone.

---

continued ...

Figure 6.2 continued

Email

Electronic text messages sent between people who are connected via a PC network, either directly or across the Internet. Electronic files can be attached to these messages, carrying any form of data (e.g. spreadsheets, word-processed documents, images, and so on).

FirstClass

An electronic mail and conferencing system.

Moderator

A person who checks the conference on a regular basis. All educational conferences should have at least one moderator. Depending on the purpose of the conference, the moderator might introduce new discussion points, respond to students and try to encourage others to participate. The moderator may also summarise, from time to time, the messages posted.

Netiquette

Netiquette (derived from net-etiquette) is the term for the etiquette governing communication on the Internet.

Non-contributor (or lurker)

This is the term for those participants in conference groups who read messages but do not (or only rarely) contribute.

Off-line

When your computer is not actively connected to the Internet. Many tutors choose to work off-line while they read and draft replies to their messages.

On-line

When your computer is actively connected (via a modem) to the Internet. Email and conference messages can only be downloaded or sent when you are on-line.

Sub-conference

This is a conference that is contained within a main conference. It is common for conferences to have sub-conferences. For example, a course-related conference might have an FAQ (frequently asked questions) sub-conference; a tutor group conference might have an 'old messages' sub-conference.

Synchronous communication

Instantaneous communication between people. This might be in a face-to-face meeting, via the telephone, or video conferencing etc. Importantly, all parties can communicate at the same time.

(adapted from the Open University (2001) internal website *Tutoring on-line: using CMC to support learning*)

INTERNET-BASED RESOURCES[3]

There is a vast array of support for student writers on the Internet, and there are numerous ways in which Internet-based resources can be used. This section surveys some of these resources, namely course websites, computer conferences, and on-line writing laboratories.

Course websites

Many institutions now place their study programmes, and descriptions of individual courses, on the web. This saves time and photocopying costs, as they can be easily updated. Some lecturers provide biblio-graphies, reading lists, and assignment outlines as well as a writing style guide, hints on appropriate academic writing for a course or subject area, sample model essays, and links to on-line study resources or journals. Course websites can also be constructed to allow students to post drafts of their writing to a site for others to read and comment upon. Unless you and your students have experience constructing and using academic websites, you may need to consult your technology support department.

Electronic computer conferencing

Electronic conferencing systems, such as the commercially available FirstClass and BlackBoard, provide a range of ways for students to com-municate with each other. Conferencing has particular advantages for developing writing: it makes available a permanent or semi-permanent record of exchanges to participants, which can be returned to after reflection; electronic writing can feed into other kinds of academic writing that students do; it can also be assessed.

In its simplest form, a conference is a series of linked discussion forums, or 'rooms', accessible to a particular group of people, that is facilitated through a computer conferencing system. Your institution may have a central conferencing system, with sub-conferences for each academic programme or faculty, each containing further sub-conferences for particular courses. Other areas on the system might be assigned for more informal communication between students (with minimum intervention from the lecturer), or for those with an interest in a specific academic topic. Figure 6.3 shows a student's conference screen.

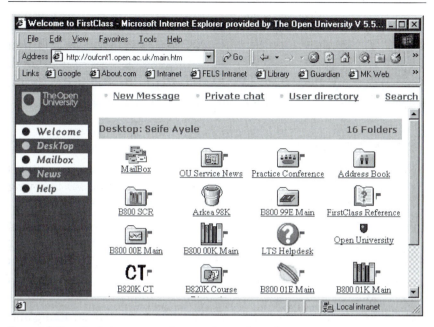

Figure 6.3 Sample desktop screen from an electronic conference

Each icon in Figure 6.3 represents a sub-conference on a particular topic, a discussion for a specific course, a place for lecturers and/or students to contact each other, or a functional space such as a mailbox. Within each sub-conference, many discussions can take place at once, some related, some unrelated. Each message posted in response to a previous message forms part of a *thread* (a series of messages on the same topic, with the same heading) which can be followed sequentially in either direction.

Figure 6.4 is taken from a cross-disciplinary postgraduate conference, where the aim is to develop students' writing through a process of peer review. Here you can see several threads as students post abstracts, literature reviews and draft proposals for their work, which are then responded to by others.[4]

Across university disciplines, electronic conferencing may be used as a means of simulating the face-to-face environment of the traditional structured tutorial or seminar – referred to in this chapter as *structured computer conferencing*. That is, the electronic conference is used as a virtual space to guide students in constructively exchanging, processing and

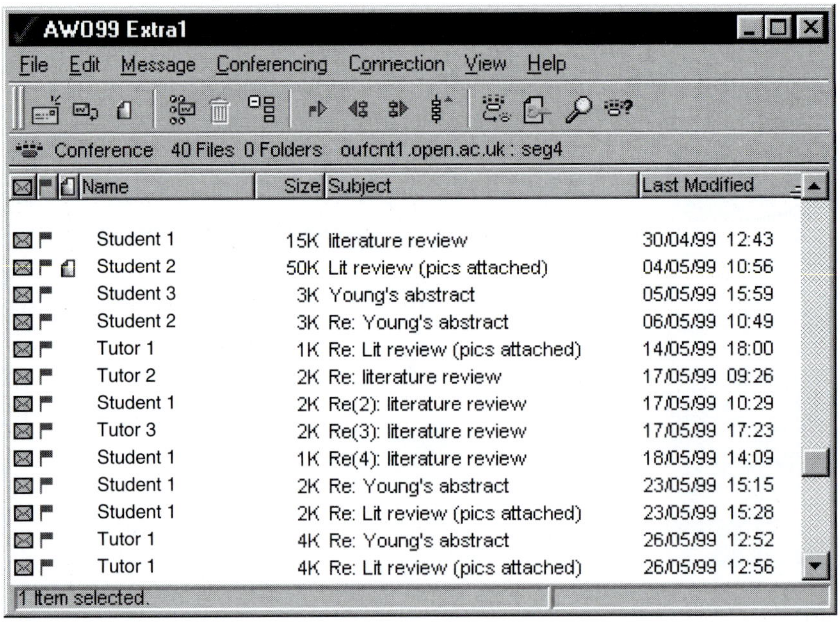

Figure 6.4 Sub-conference showing individual messages and discussion threads

synthesising ideas, theories and research findings. Electronic conferencing can either have as its aim the teaching of disciplinary knowledge, or the aim can be academic writing itself. Later in this chapter we consider how academic discussion via a computer can contribute to the development of students' ability to write in an academic style.

There are two main ways of using computer conferencing: *synchronous communication*, where the students are on-line at the same time for a tutorial, or *asynchronous communication*, where students log in when it is convenient and read and respond to posted messages. Many courses use a mixture of both synchronous and asynchronous systems: conferences are open for discussion all the time, and/or certain tasks may be set to be carried out over, say, a week. On particular dates a structured tutorial may take place, or an academic expert from another institution can be invited to give a presentation on-line and answer questions.

Electronic conferencing: practical issues

- Course conferences can be set up using independent software which all students load onto their computer,[5] or they can be accessed from a central course or university website. It is usually simpler to use a website, particularly if you have students in different countries, as this obviates the need for special software. On the other hand, using software can provide better technical quality.

- There is little evidence that real savings can be achieved through electronic tuition – maintaining quality in the medium can in fact cost more than traditional face-to-face teaching (Breen *et al.*, 2001).

- The design of a conference, and the way it is introduced to students is crucial to its success. Salmon (2000) has developed a five-stage model for setting up student conferencing and reflecting on the issues involved (see annotated bibliography). Students unused to electronic conferencing may require a sensitive process of induction, especially if the student group is geographically dispersed. 'Ice-breaker' activities can be helpful, encouraging students to participate, discuss their apprehension and help dispel any sense of isolation.

On-line Writing Laboratories

On-line Writing Laboratories (OWLs; sometimes called On-line Writing Centers) are primarily resource sites and come mainly from the United States.[6] They provide a range of services for writers and lecturers: some allow students to contact specialist writing tutors via email; most have some form of conferencing system; all have resources for writers either from their institution's website or links to external sites. Often these resources for writing can be downloaded (transferred to your own computer) and used directly with students; or adapted to your particular purpose. OWLs also provide detailed guides to the process of writing, including guides to grammar, spelling, punctuation, and exemplars of academic and other writing styles. There are guides to writing email and appropriate behaviour on the web (netiquette). Such models are useful for less confident or inexperienced writers, and for students with English as an additional language who may need to familiarise themselves with new academic conventions. Some areas within an OWL are restricted to students and lecturers registered at the host institution. However, many OWL resources are freely accessible on the World Wide Web. These are well worth browsing for ideas, and you can encourage your students to evaluate them and discuss how they might use the information they contain.

Figure 6.5 is an extract from Purdue University's OWL, explaining to students the difference between passive and active voice. It is part of a wide-ranging collection of handouts on various aspects of student writing, from punctuation to essay structure.

Figure 6.5 Extract from a downloadable handout on Purdue University's OWL

Choosing active voice

In most non-scientific writing situations, active voice is preferable to passive for the majority of your sentences. Even in scientific writing, overuse of passive voice or use of passive voice in long and complicated sentences can cause readers to lose interest or to become confused. Sentences in active voice are generally – though not always – clearer and more direct than those in passive voice.

passive (indirect)	*active (direct)*
The entrance exam *was failed* by over one-third of the applicants to the school.	Over one-third of the applicants to the school *failed* the entrance exam.
The brakes *were slammed on* by her as the car sped downhill.	She *slammed on* the brakes as the car sped downhill.
Your bicycle *has been damaged*.	I *have damaged* your bicycle.

(http://owl.english.purdue.edu/)

As you read the extract in Figure 6.5, it may be useful to consider the extent to which this general advice about the use of passive voice takes into account disciplinary differences, as discussed in Chapter 3. How useful would it be for your particular students?

Another OWL activity is to use a conference as a site for lecturers and peers to comment on examples of students' writing (see Chapter 2 on peer review). Figure 6.6 shows some sample messages from the Academic Writing On-line conference illustrated in Figure 6.4. This conference aims at improving the academic writing of postgraduate students specifically in relation to the conventions of preparing abstracts, literature reviews and conference papers. The first message on the left is from a student who has posted his abstract in draft form to the conference for others to read and comment on. A couple of days later, a tutor responds with the message on the right.

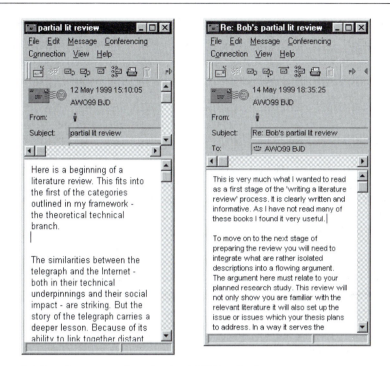

Figure 6.6 Sample messages from Academic Writing On-line course

Evaluating Internet information

For discipline-specific resources such as on-line journal articles on academic topics, and a wealth of other resources useful to both teachers and students researching essay topics (e.g. encyclopaedias and discussion forums), the web's search engines can be used. A good guide to using the Internet for research purposes can be found at the University of Toronto (http://www.erin.utoronto.ca/~w3lib/pub/evaluate/webevalu.htm). Beginners on the Internet can also use on-line tutorials to learn how to find information effectively: see, for example, the University of California at Berkeley (http://www.lib.berkeley.edu/TeachingLib/Guides/Internet/FindInfo.html).

Students need to learn to be critical of the information they find on the Internet, asking questions such as: what is its source, what is the status of the information, who is the author and why did she or he write it? A good starting point is the self-access tutorial Internet Detective (http://www.sosig.ac.uk/desire/internet-detective.html), which novice Internet users can use to train themselves in the important art of evaluating on-line sources. Other sites also aim to encourage a critical orientation to information found on-line. The checklist in Figure 6.7 is taken from the University of Wisconsin Library's website (http:// www.library. wisc.edu/libraries/Instruction/instmat/webeval.htm), and shows the sort of questions students can be encouraged to ask.

Figure 6.7 Evaluating websites

Checklist for evaluating websites

Authority • *Who/what organisation* is responsible for this site?
Look for a header or footer that indicates organisational affiliation.
Look for a link to the home page of the website where the document lives.
• Can you find *author's qualifications on the subject*?
Look for 'About the author/About us' links on the page.
• Can you *verify information* (another source, address, phone number in addition to email address)?
Look at domain of the URL.[7] Example: .gov in the URL means it's a government site.
Look for name, address, phone number in addition to email address.
Look in another source, e.g. phone book, encyclopedia, reference book.
Purpose • What is the *purpose* of the page? *To inform? Persuade? Sell? Entertain?*
Look for 'About us/Mission/Purpose' links on the page itself.
Go to the home page of the site (use a link if possible, or back up in the URL) and look for 'About us/Mission/Purpose' links there.
• Any potential for *bias, especially if site is trying to provide information as well as sell something*?
Look at content to see if it is just an 'infomercial'.
Are ads *distinct from informational content*?

With some guidance and practice, students can become adept at integrating information found on the Internet into their writing. We turn now to a more detailed discussion of electronic conferencing in the context of teaching disciplinary knowledge and consider how the medium can be used to develop students' understanding and control of academic writing.

USING ELECTRONIC CONFERENCING TO DEVELOP STUDENTS' ACADEMIC WRITING

This section is divided into two subsections. First we consider the written exchanges that occur as part of structured electronic conferencing. We then consider their relationship with individually written assessment tasks.

Writing as part of structured conferencing

Unlike face-to-face tutorials and seminars, electronic conferencing requires lecturers and students to use the written, rather than spoken, word as the chief medium of communication. Although this form of written exchange may differ from more formal styles of academic writing (such as those explored in Chapter 3), it is nevertheless an important vehicle for learning to express abstract ideas and for exchanging views on disciplinary knowledge. Therefore it is useful to consider the nature and role of such exchanges and to explore their relationship with more traditional, individually produced, academic text types (such as the argument essay – see Chapters 2 and 3).

Currently it is difficult to accurately and comprehensively characterise the language of written electronic exchange as the medium is still in its infancy (though developing rapidly) and its potential as a teaching and learning tool has yet to be fully realised. An important feature of writing as part of computer conferencing is that it is not a homogenous entity. As in face-to-face contexts, writing used in electronic conferencing varies according to the purpose of the writing, the subject matter and the relationship between those making the exchanges. For example, chats in virtual cafés and coffee bars and other informal sub-conferences, where the relationship between peers is generally equal, are more likely to simulate the spoken styles of face-to-face conversation than are more formal structured conferences. This informality is often reflected in the absence of full grammatical sentences, a decrease in concern about punctuation and a high tolerance for typographic and spelling errors (see Chapter 2 for a discussion on informal/formal writing).

Degrees of formality and informality in writing also vary according to the stage in the sequence of teaching and learning. For example, in the introductory stages of structured electronic conferencing, lecturers frequently spend time familiarising students with the nature of electronic conferencing. Another common aim at this point is to foster a sense of belonging to a virtual community.

Figure 6.8 outlines some common strategies for developing a sense of community, followed by comments on the implications for writing style. How could these strategies be used with your particular students, if they are new to electronic conferencing?

Figure 6.8 Strategies for creating an on-line community

Strategies for creating an on-line community

- Lecturers and students write a short introductory message covering work, leisure activities or academic interests.
- Students are divided into pairs or small groups and interview each other (using email or sub-conferences) to find out each other's hopes and fears about the course and/or the role of electronic conferencing.
- Lecturers send a message suggesting a set of simple ground rules for developing and maintaining manageable and effective on-line communication (see Activity 6.1 for a suggested list). Each student has to agree or disagree with the message and suggest any additional ground rules that they think would contribute to constructive interaction, e.g. acknowledging previous contributions before adding their own messages, using threads to develop a particular line of thought.
- Lecturers solicit ground rules from students rather than proposing them.
- Lecturers use ground rules to make explicit protocols and conventions of electronic conferencing as a means of highlighting the rather different purposes and styles of on-line writing compared to more formal writing tasks.
- Lecturers provide models of more and less formal writing from electronic conferencing and ask students to compare the register of these forms of writing with target text types (such as a case study or argument essay) in their discipline area.

Students could be given the list in Figure 6.8 as a handout or email and asked which rules would contribute to more productive interaction and learning in their particular context. The list of ground rules in Activity 6.1 could be posted to a conference, as suggested in several of the strategies listed in Figure 6.8. At the start of a conference, a chatty, friendly approach is more likely to encourage students to feel part of a social (rather than just academic) community. As a result students are likely to make spontaneous contributions that take less time and warrant less analysis and reflection than do more academically related knowledge exchanges.

Activity 6.1 Establishing ground rules for conferencing

- Generally, try to use an informal style of writing, for example use first person voice (*I, we*), contractions (e.g. *it's, I'll*) and colloquial language (e.g. *Hi there! I'm getting back to Paul's message where he argued that…*) where appropriate.

- Be careful what you say to or about others. (Conferences are more public than email.)

- Thank, acknowledge and support people freely.

- Don't 'shout' by typing in capital letters.

- Read through your posting carefully to make sure your message can not be misinterpreted.

- Acknowledge fellow students' views before differing.

- Before you respond to a message where you strongly disagree with the views expressed, pause and reflect.

- Make clear whether you are speaking from your own or an acknowledged other perspective.

- Lift and quote from the messages of others before replying.

- Ensure that you place new messages in the appropriate conference.

- Use a short, effective title for your message.

- When replying to someone else's message, use the same title if the subject remains the same as before, otherwise start a new thread with a new title.

- Where possible, keep messages short – ideally never more than one screenful. (This will facilitate a dialogue with other people. Long monologues are difficult to read on screen.)

- Break a text into short paragraphs where possible (it will be easier to read).

- If you want to say or share anything longer than one screenful in a message, attach a document. (Make sure that recipients have suitable software to download and open the document. Use a rich text format (.rtf) version where appropriate.)

- Use several messages for different topics (this aids replying).

(expanded and adapted from Salmon, 2000: 159)

If students are new to electronic conferencing, it may be helpful to make clear that an informal style of writing is acceptable and that messages do not need to read like carefully written essays. Modelling an informal, interactive style, as illustrated in Figure 6.9, can play a particularly important role in showing students what is expected.

Figure 6.9 Modelling an informal style

Hi everyone

I think so far your contributions have been really interesting. I thought Andrew's idea for a ground rule to stop any one student dominating a discussion was especially important. Jane, I liked your point about this as well. What do other people think? Do you generally agree with the idea that…

In the introductory stages of electronic conferencing, particularly if students are unfamiliar with the medium, useful linguistic structures and phrases can be introduced for later use, drawing attention to the need for both lecturers and students to compensate for the absence of non-verbal and visual clues by giving explicit feedback on each other's contributions (e.g. *I liked your point about this*).

Likewise, lecturers may need to highlight the need to ask open questions in order to facilitate interaction. Some examples of useful structures and phrases are illustrated (in italics) in the following interaction in which students studying a masters in business administration exchange ideas on stakeholders (Figure 6.10). Model electronic exchanges such as these can be used with students to exemplify the kinds of interaction that you wish to promote. Ideally these models should be taken from your discipline area.

After the ice-breaking and awareness-raising activities of the introductory stages of an electronic conference, the focus generally develops into a discussion of the topics, theories and research that comprise the particular programme of study. Academic debates will not, however, emerge naturally. Without some kind of structure, students may stay at the 'chatty' level.

Developing a virtual environment in which all students feel sufficiently comfortable and confident to test their understanding of, and ideas about, academic knowledge is not straightforward. Unlike in a face-to-face environment where participants' contributions are ephemeral, written exchanges are frozen in time and can be analysed in greater depth, thus

Figure 6.10 Model text illustrating effective electronic conferencing

---

Message 1

Thanks to all who have so far responded to my plea for ideas on stakeholders. Please keep your thoughts coming!

How significant are 'lenders' to the voluntary sector? Do voluntary organisations take out loans like private companies, and end up having to raise funds to pay bank interest?

And who is the competition? Is there direct head on competition like Pepsi and Coke?

Or is it more sideways competition, competing for lottery money or for the pound in my pocket against other things I might spend it on?

Regards Paul

Message 2

Paul asks 'who is the competition?'

I think competition in the VOLUNTARY SECTOR comes in several forms: Rival fund-raising activities, rival bids for contracts, rival bids for grants eg the national lottery, other service providers, selling its products merchandise (charity shops), education, I'm sure there's more!! *Does that help?*

Cara

(Salmon, 2000: 149)

---

laying students open to greater critique. Non-native speakers of English may also find it hard contributing to a conference if there are too many culturally bound references or specialist terms. Setting up an on-line discipline-specific glossary may, however, solve the latter problem.

For some students, however, the written medium can be quite liberating. For example, there are clear benefits for non-native speakers of English and shy students in general in having time to read, digest, reflect, and respond to others in asynchronous communication compared with face-to-face classrooms or synchronous chat. In asynchronous electronic conferencing, there is less pressure 'to get the floor' and students can develop a discussion in a number of directions. One student makes this point well:

> Somebody was saying because they'd been able to sit and think it out and write it out it was more solid as it were…Whereas if they'd just been talking they wouldn't have had the luxury of a fifteen minute monologue…you don't get that sort of concentrated putting across a point of view when you have a face to face discussion.
>
> (Lea, 2001: 167)

In order to encourage student participation you will probably need to use structured activities in addition to more open discussion. Structured activities can be used to focus on both disciplinary knowledge and writing. For example, in order to encourage academic debate, you could adapt one of the strategies in Figure 6.11. These strategies are designed to give students practice in rehearsing academic arguments which in turn can make writing an argument essay easier (as discussed in more detail later in this section).

Figure 6.11 Developing academic argument in an electronic conference

Developing academic argument in an electronic conference: some strategies

A. During a discussion on a particular topic, allocate students a task in order to develop and practise their repertoire of argumentative strategies. Tasks could include:

- questioning and challenging a theory or idea
- taking up an alternative perspective on an issue
- drawing on evidence which counters another student's point
- critiquing evidence put forward by another student
- endorsing a previous argument/use of evidence
- extending a previous argument/adding evidence
- clarifying an ambiguous argument/use of evidence
- summarising the overall arguments put forward.

B. At the end of an electronic discussion, as an awareness activity, ask students to identify the argumentative strategies that they used (such as those listed in strategy A above). Discuss with them the effectiveness of their exchange.

C. Divide students into groups (by using sub-conferences) and ask each group to gather and synthesise evidence for a particular argument/point of view on an issue. Each group puts up their contribution on the conference site and the lecturer guides the students in integrating the evidence to form a coherent argument essay. Equally you could ask students to use the different arguments in formulating their own off-line essay.

D. As part of an assessment strategy ask students to contribute at least two messages to the conference and/or reference their fellow-students' electronic messages in a written essay.

Figure 6.12 Activity from MA in Open and Distance Education H805, Open
University

Tutor Group Activity 2: Higher Education in the Developing World

Start: 16 February 2002 – End: 1 March 2002
Before you start this on-line tutor group activity you should have:

- Read through the Block 1 Study Guide, sections 2 and 3 (pp. 11–31).
- Read through Readings 1 and 2 (Perraton, Chapters 1 and 5).
- Successfully logged on to your Tutor Group conference and read some of the messages that others have sent, and sent at least one of your own.

During the course of the two-week activity we expect that you will also be working through Readings 3, 4, 5 and 6 (Perraton, Chapter 7; Jakupec and Garrick, Chapters 1, 4 and 6), and that you will use them to inform the activity.

The activity is a structured on-line debate on the topic 'Open and Distance Education has failed to meet the expectations that were envisaged for educational expansion and access'. It is intended to help you start to use the course materials and resources to clarify the issues that are considered central to this subject and, at the same time, to give you some practice in formulating your own ideas as part of an interactive textual dialogue with your colleagues.

The activity should involve you for three to six hours over the two-week period: reading others' messages; writing your own; and doing the tasks associated with the role you are assigned.

Task

If you check in your tutor group conference, you will see that you have been allocated to either the 'for' or 'against' group and given a specific role to play in the debate. Please refer to the explanation of the duties of the various roles (below). We hope that, regardless of your real opinion, you will enter into the spirit of the role you have been allocated and play your part accordingly!

The topic (or motion) of the debate is:

Open and Distance Education has failed to meet the expectations that were envisaged for educational expansion and access.

Here are the roles and associated tasks for the debate.

Proposer of the motion: the proposer's role is to put a short message (no more than one screenful) into the activity conference, arguing that the statement is true, in such a way as to encourage comment from participants.

Opposer: the opposer's role is to counter the proposer's message by putting in a message of similar length arguing for the opposite point of view, again in such a way as to encourage further comment.

continued ...

Figure 6.12 continued

Documentalist: the two documentalists' role is to send a message summarising one or more of the set readings for Block 1, picking out the points relevant to the motion, both for and against.

Researcher: the researcher's role is to make a short list of other readings, extracts and resources (from the Study Guide, the Set Books, and the web) that are relevant to the motion, and bring them to the attention of the group.

Summariser for the motion: the summariser (for) role involves sending a message at the end of the activity, which summarises the case in favour of the motion and urges participants to vote for!

Summariser against the motion: the summariser (against) role involves sending a message at the end of the activity, which summarises the case against the motion and urges participants to vote against!

Commenters: the commenters' role is allocated to everyone to perform in addition to their main role. It is to respond to ideas put forward by all of the above and help keep a discussion going. There is no restriction on the number of messages you can send, but please keep them as concise as you can.

Approximate sequence of events
1   Proposer's and Opposer's initial statements
2   Comments in response
3   Documentalists' summaries
4   Comments in response
5   Researcher's lists
6   Free-for-all discussion
7   Summarisers' statements
8   Vote

Figure 6.12 is an example of how a masters course adapted and implemented the strategies in Figure 6.11. It shows the instructions given to students as part of an activity focusing on higher education in the developing world.

Which strategy(ies) for encouraging academic debate do you think would work in your particular context? What do you see as the advantages and the pitfalls?

As students progress from engaging primarily in activities designed to build a social community towards participating in structured academic discussion, it is important to maintain a friendly, personal style. However, whilst introductory activities may warrant immediate, spontaneous thoughts, academically focused interaction requires a different balance of the spontaneous and the considered. This may result in a style of exchange that has features of more formal, academic writing.

It is therefore important for lecturers to present a suitable style for students familiar with the informal styles of spoken interaction and the formal styles of academic writing, but not necessarily sure of what voice to adopt in an electronic conference. That is, although electronic communication has yet to develop a stable, easily definable style, research suggests that it is a hybrid form, incorporating features from both the spoken and written (Halliday, 1996). In Activity 6.2 there are two extracts that could be used with students to highlight these differences. Extract A is taken from an electronic conference, whereas Extract B is taken from a written argument essay. Both form part of a history programme. (You may of course want to use examples from your own discipline.) In Extract A, it would be useful to comment on the following features:

- The participants directly address each other, either by name or the general *you*, and thus invite an ongoing exchange of opinions and ideas.
- Personal views are expressed explicitly and language is often colloquial and informal.
- Questions and responses to questions are common strategies.

In Extract B it would be useful to comment on these features:

- The writer is not able to directly name and address his or her audience given that they are possibly unknown and certainly distant in time and place.
- The language is formal and relatively 'compressed' (with a high frequency of dense, nominal groups, some of which we have italicised as examples).
- The writer does not directly intrude into the text to offer his or her opinion.
- There are no questions and no use of personal pronouns (e.g. *I* and *you*).

The above examples highlight some of the differences between writing produced when working together on-line, and writing produced in the more traditional solitary way. The next section looks at the relationship between the two.

Activity 6.2 Comparing forms of academic argument

Extract A *Writing together on-line* Contributions to an electronic conference discussing the extent to which Stalinism was the inevitable outcome of the Bolshevik Revolution.	*Extract B* *Writing alone* The final paragraph of a formal argument essay in which the writer puts forward a position in relation to the essay question 'Was Stalinism the inevitable outcome of the Bolshevik Revolution?'

Message 7 (Fathima):

Hi there everyone In his last message Joe said that it was inevitable that Stalinism was the outcome of the revolution. I don't really agree with this. I can see why some of your arguments make sense, Joe, but I think you're missing a major point i.e. in my view Stalinism came about because of Stalin himself. In other words, Stalin was an extraordinarily ambitious individual and his particular political cunning was the reason for 'Stalinism'. I guess this ties in with my general theory of history – people and not just abstract long term 'historical' conditions can have a major impact on how societies work/ don't work.

What does everyone else think?

Reply to Message 7 (Anne):

Hello all! I have read your comments, Fathima. Personally, I am a bit unsure of your viewpoint. As you say, it's partly a result of your more general view of history which I'm not sure I agree with. But now I'm beginning to think that maybe in some ways you have a point. It's true that Stalin himself was extremely powerful. I think mainly because of his political cunning in making himself an indispensable cog in the government's machinery. I still think the revolution had a powerful role in enabling Stalin to rise through the ranks but then maybe he couldn't have made the ascent without his particular political savvy and willingness to take on lots of boring, dull jobs. I'd be really interested to know what the rest of the group think and especially Paul, as tutor????

Essay – final paragraph:

Stalinism resulted from a combination of factors, chief of which was *the party's oversight in failing to provide an adequate leadership structure. Any political party which fails to devise a method of choosing its leader and to place limits of power and tenure on that leader* leaves itself open to dictatorship. The combination of policies, dictated by events as much as ideology, the over-centralising of power, and *the socio-historic background of Russia itself*, all contributed. Stalinism was not an *inevitable result of the Bolshevik revolution*, but rather *a result of the Bolshevik party's oversights in strategic areas which allowed one man's political ambition and cunning to gain him absolute power.* (Roberts, 1997: 86)

Writing in structured conferencing and writing for assessment – the relationship

In the previous section we saw how, although electronic conferencing in itself provides practice in writing, the writing skills used by students and lecturers in academic exchange are different to those required in traditional, individually written, academic assignments. We also saw that as conferences progress from being primarily social in orientation to being academically focused, contributions become less casual and spontaneous. This is particularly the case if students value the exchange as a permanent record of a debate which they can return to as a source of information and ideas for their written assignments. Such academic exchanges may lead to students taking more time to reflect. They may often prepare contributions off-line, re-drafting and editing texts, before the final considered product is posted to the conference.

In the previous section we also suggested that activities such as participating in debates, rehearsing arguments and critically analysing a range of different perspectives and views foster the kinds of discursive skills necessary for successful written argumentation. In other words, activities in which students take up and support or counter (with evidence) different perspectives on a topic, develop a written record of the various positions that a student can then draw on in writing an essay. Students have made the following points about this process:

> It was invaluable to see how different people took things on board, and it made you think outside your own little box, and push these ideas into new sorts of areas.
>
> It's useful for making you consolidate your ideas, finalise them almost, to say where you have reached, even if it's just a list. It doesn't have to be strung together sentences … I think I personally attain a different level of depth when I write that I don't attain when I'm talking …
>
> (Lea, 2001: 167)

Not only does electronic conferencing support the rehearsal of a range of views and perspectives, it can also serve as a rhetorical resource for students' written assignments. That is, a practice that is developing on some on-line courses is for students to incorporate the electronic messages of fellow students (through direct quotation or paraphrasing) into their writing, for example, as evidence for their arguments. This is particularly the case in applied programmes which value the practical experience of professionals in the field (for example, education and business courses). In some courses this practice is made obligatory with assignment tasks including instructions such as:

> In this assignment marks will be given for including at least three messages from the debate in your electronic conferencing group, and for commenting on key points made in the debate.
>
> As part of the review, compare some of the factors that the authors highlight with your own experience as a teacher and/or learner. You should also draw on the comments that other students make about this topic in your electronic conference.
>
> (adapted from an Open University Masters in Applied Linguistics course)

Some students benefit by engaging directly with conference messages which present an array of different perspectives. The process appears to facilitate the integration of peers' messages, texts and ideas into their individually written text to support or counter the writer's own position. However, not all students find it easy to make the required linkage between writing in an electronic conference and writing an essay. For example, some see the process of integrating other students' messages into their own essays as a rather contrived, artificial process (and merely a practice designed to make obligatory their participation in conferencing). They may find it difficult to manage the different levels of authority and expertise when integrating references from peers with references from established authorities. Likewise, lecturers may find it problematic for students' conference messages to be invested with the authority normally reserved for established authors. As Lea points out:

> traditional academic convention might expect the work of the recognised and authoritative published author to be foregrounded, and experiential or anecdotal evidence provided by the student to illustrate the authoritative evidence.
>
> (Lea, 2001: 174)

However, she also notes that in relation to a postgraduate on-line course in the relatively new and evolving field of open and distance education, students seem to be at ease in foregrounding their own debates and experiences rather than those of a recognised authority.

This points to the need for lecturers to develop clear conventions that are appropriate both in terms of the teaching and learning goals of the programme and in terms of the expectations of the disciplinary community at large.

The problem of incorporating electronic messages into formal written tasks is compounded by the paucity of models for such writing. One solution is to provide sample texts where students have successfully incorporated their peers' electronic messages to strengthen their argument. Another is to vary the assignments that accompany on-line courses so that essays (and other traditional text types) are not the only form of assessment. Salmon (2000: 92), for example, notes the paradox of students using electronic conferencing and word-processing to carry out a major part of their learning and then sitting for traditional exams that restrict them to using pen and paper in a formal setting.

TECHNOLOGY AND ASSESSMENT

This section considers the impact of technology on referencing conventions, the relationship between technology and plagiarism and the increasing use of multimedia assignments.

Referencing on-line publications, conference messages and websites

Universities have clear policies on citation and acknowledgement of sources, but these may still assume a book culture based around a traditional library. Copyright is a notoriously complicated subject, and nowhere more so than on the Internet. Lecturers need to agree their expectations on referencing and citation with students at the start, and ensure that they understand that images and audio-visual material, as well as text, are covered by copyright law. A simple convention for referencing websites is:

Author, initials, (year) title, medium, date. Available from: URL of website [date the site was accessed].

The conventions for referencing electronic messages may vary considerably and it is necessary to make explicit the particular university or course's requirements. Here is an example:

Luff, R. (2001) 'Questionnaire', on-line posting to FirstClass conference, 20 August. Available from: http://oufcnt1.open.ac.uk/main.htm [Accessed 24 August 2001].

Some universities produce guides to citing electronic sources in academic writing – for example Bournemouth University (http://www.bournemouth.ac.uk/using_the_library/html/guide_to_citing_internet_sourc.html), which has suggestions for citing emails as well as information found on websites. A detailed guide to referencing on-line sources in different citation systems (Chicago, MLA, etc.) can be found at *online!* (http://www.bedfordstmartins.com/online/).

Technology and plagiarism

As discussed in Chapter 4, plagiarism is difficult to define. Many of the examples of near-plagiarism appearing in student essays may be due to uncertainty about academic writing conventions, lack of confidence, or other factors (Goodman, 2002; Pennycook, 1996). Deliberate cheating happens, however; the same conditions that facilitate retrieval of information and student discussion can be used to make plagiarism easier. An ever-increasing number of electronic sources of student texts is also available. Essays can be easily transmitted between students as an email attachment or on disk, and once received can be copied, or altered to fit requirements such as a revised essay title. From the Internet, students can download short paragraphs from journal articles, book reviews and encyclopaedias – or entire essays on a subject (put the term 'essay bank' or 'term paper' into a search engine for examples of sites offering complete essays, for commission or free of charge). If essays are paid for, students can specify the standard of writing and grade required, to reduce the chances of getting caught.

The same tools that make it easier to plagiarise, however, also make plagiarism easier to detect. For do-it-yourself detection, some time and lateral thinking are required. You may spot similarities between essays, or have your suspicions raised by an inconsistent writing style, paragraphs which don't seem to follow on from one another, patches of writing with

American spelling between parts with British spelling, out-of-date references, etc. If you have the time and the inclination, a quick way of checking whether unattributed electronic sources have been used is to put a short phrase from the essay into a search engine. Choosing a slightly unusual phrase will be more expedient as fewer 'hits' will be returned. Checking entire essays, however, is time consuming; you may find it easier to use commercial software designed to detect plagiarism. There are many packages available, some claiming to use advanced linguistic techniques to identify plagiarised text or collaboration between groups of students. An introduction to detection programmes is available in a report from Sheffield University (Clough, 2000). Some resources, such as those provided by Plagiarism.org (www.plagiarism.org) run student essays through a check which trawls the Internet essay banks looking for similarities. Others, such as Copycatch (http://www.copycatch. freeserve.co.uk/vocalyse.htm) developed at Birmingham University, aim to check for collusion between groups of students. Clough's report (2000) gives details on how each detection programme works, although to date there is no definitive data about which programme is better, and which suits which purposes best (probably due to the difficulty in obtaining sufficient plagiarised assignments for testing). However, a project looking at student plagiarism in British universities is underway (see the Annotated bibliography).

There is clearly a tension here between encouraging students to use the Internet as a resource and for communicating with each other, and becoming anxious about plagiarism. You will have to decide for yourself and agree with your students on the type of work they are required to do, what use is to be made of external sources, and how sources are to be referenced.

Multimedia assignments

It is worth considering using the available technology not only to enhance how students work and learn, but to provide them with wider options in their assignments. Essays drawing on Internet sources are likely to include links to URLs which lecturers can follow if the essays are submitted electronically; students can also include images, video clips and audio material in their work. Shephard (2001) advocates the use of multimedia as an alternative to traditional text for assignment submission. It allows for the inclusion of visual or numerical data which can be difficult to convey adequately in words. Shephard also cites evidence that multimedia work can enhance the understanding and learning process, and can be highly motivating for students. Compact disks (now very cheap) can be used for this purpose, and information downloadable onto them can be found on the Internet (many images, for example, are freely available). Assignments can include scanned photographs, audio recordings of interviews, and digital video recordings. As with all electronically submitted assignments, you will need to consider how you will mark them, as without at least a laptop computer they will not be as portable as hard copy. Experience also shows that more time is generally needed for marking in this way.

CONCLUSION

Having surveyed a range of ways in which technology can be used to facilitate or improve students' academic writing, let us return to our initial scenario, that of the lecturer wishing to develop an on-line course for the first time. The first port of call should probably be the university's computing department and/or writing centre if this exists, as there may be some expertise available, particularly in setting up the technical side of things. But a do-it-yourself approach is certainly possible, drawing on the vast resources already available on-line, and adapting these to your specific needs and objectives. In the case of Sarah, the lecturer, she could first clarify with students how computers can help them to develop their academic writing skills. She could also enlist the help of the following:

- OWL handouts
- the Internet, with its numerous writing resources
- an electronic conference for developing students' argument skills
- email for assignment submission.

It is important for the lecturer to provide support in making the most of these possibilities. Technology does not replace the lecturer, but provides a rich resource which can be used to great effect if incorporated thoughtfully.

NOTES

1 At the time of going to press, the website addresses given in this book were correct. Due to the ephemeral nature of websites, however, we cannot guarantee that these will still be operational in future. To locate a new website address or find an alternative go to a search engine such as www.altavista.com or www.google.com, and type in the name of the university, journal, etc. you are looking for. For more general searches, type in a search phrase such as 'evaluating on-line resources', remembering to enclose your phrase in double quotation marks to search for an exact match.

2 A Listserv is a discussion forum on a particular topic. You can subscribe via the Internet or a Listserv may be run through an institution such as a university. Once subscribed, you may then post messages, which are sent to all subscribers via normal email. Listservs can be ideal when participants are geographically scattered and/or have no access to technology other than a basic email account.

3 Strictly speaking, the Internet refers to the multiple networks of computers linked electronically to each other around the world (the infrastructure) whereas the World Wide Web is a facility on that infrastructure. The web accounts for the majority of Internet use, however, and increasingly the two terms are used interchangeably.

4 Names of participants have been removed for reasons of privacy.

5 Sheffield University hosts a website commenting on a wide variety of CMC resources and software, with illustrative links for visitors to explore the different programmes for themselves (http://collaborate.shef.ac.uk/resources.html).

6 See, for example, http://owl.english.purdue.edu/; or
http://writing.richmond.edu/writing/.

7 URL = universal resource locator, known as a website address.

Annotated bibliography

CHAPTER I

Angelil-Carter, S. (ed.) (1998) *Access to Success. Literacy in Academic Contexts*, Cape Town: University of Cape Town Press.

An edited collection of papers written by researchers and practitioners in the highly complex and dynamic higher education context of South Africa. The papers deal with policy, pedagogy and theories of student writing, and are grounded in the everyday experiences of students and teachers in higher education.

Lea, M.R. and Street, B.V. (1998) 'Student writing in higher education: an academic literacies approach', *Studies in Higher Education* 23(2): 157–72.

Lea and Street introduce their now widely cited 'three models' approach to student writing in higher education. These models are defined as 'study skills', 'academic socialisation' and 'academic literacies', each of which is outlined in the paper. Whilst the first two models are prevalent in higher education, they argue that it is the third, 'academic literacies' model which should be informing research and pedagogy in higher education.

Zamel, V. and Spack, R. (eds) (1998) *Negotiating Academic Literacies: Teaching and Learning across Languages and Cultures*, Mahwah, NJ: Lawrence Erlbaum.

An edited collection of seminal research on student writing by both native and non-native speakers of English. Covers topics including essayist literacy, assessment, plagiarism, and the politics of language in the academy.

CHAPTER 2

Crème, P. and Lea, M.R. (1997) *Writing at University: A Guide for Students*, Buckingham: Open University Press.

This book is designed as a guide for students but includes many activities which could usefully be adapted for use in lectures and tutorials designed to ease students into writing in higher education.

Ferris, D. and Hedgcock, J.S. (1998) *Teaching ESL Composition: Purpose, Process, and Practice*, Mahwah, NJ and London: Lawrence Erlbaum.

An exhaustive compendium of issues related to teaching academic writing to non-native speakers of English. Includes theoretical and practical elements including the reading and writing relationship and designing lessons, teaching activities and reflection exercises.

Northedge, A. (1990) *The Good Study Guide*, Milton Keynes: The Open University.

Northedge, A., Thomas J., Lane, A. and Peasgood, A. (1997) *The Sciences Good Study Guide*, Milton Keynes: The Open University.

Both these books are designed for undergraduate students and cover not only writing but reading, note taking, working with numbers and taking examinations. They provide a useful broader picture if your students are having assignment related problems.

Swales, J. and Feak, C. (1994) *Academic Writing for Graduate Students*, Ann Arbor: University of Michigan Press.

Swales, J. and Feak, C. (2000) *English in Today's Research World*, Ann Arbor: University of Michigan Press.

Excellent books for non-native English-speaking postgraduates with activities that raise awareness about linguistic and rhetorical aspects of academic writing as well as the communicative demands of the larger academic context.

CHAPTER 3

Halliday, M.A.K. and Martin, J.R. (1993) *Writing Science: Literary and Discursive Power*, London: Falmer Press.

There is a body of work that has largely evolved in the Australian context which includes Halliday and Martin's work on science and Wignell's work on the social sciences/sociology. These exemplify how linguistics can be used to make explicit how language functions to create knowledge differently in different disciplines.

MacDonald, S.P. (1994) *Professional Academic Writing in the Humanities and Social Sciences*, Carbondale and Edwardsville, IL: Southern Illinois University Press.

This book examines published writing in branches of psychology, history and literary studies in order to make clearer the paradigms they are working within and how these are manifest in writing practices. This is not a practical book, but one which deepens understanding of the complexity of knowledge creation in different fields.

Wignell, P. (1998) 'Technicality and abstraction in social science', in J.R. Martin and R. Veel (eds) *Reading Science: Critical and Functional Perspectives on Discourses of Science*, London: Routledge. See entry under Halliday and Martin above.

CHAPTER 4

Brown, G., Bull, J. and Pendlebury, M. (1997) *Assessing Student Learning in Higher Education*, London: Routledge.

Aimed at teachers in higher education, this book is a good source not only of ideas but of research conducted into different types of learning and assessment. A main focus is on how the type of assessment affects the type of learning students engage in. It covers a wide range of assessment types (essays, projects, self- and peer assessment, portfolios, multiple choice, practical work, oral presentations). Each chapter has activities at the end designed to help readers focus on and improve their own assessment practice, with notes on these at the end of the book. A Further Reading section is provided, dealing with different aspects of assessment, as well as a comprehensive bibliography.

Brown, S. and Glasner, A. (eds) (1999) *Assessment Matters in Higher Education: Choosing and Using Diverse Approaches*, Buckingham: The Society for Research into Higher Education and Open University Press.

Edited collection of chapters dealing mainly with the 'what', 'why' and 'how' of assessment. The book is divided into four parts. The first deals with systems approaches to assessment (institution-wide strategies); the second looks at innovative assessment and its effectiveness; the third considers the assessment of practice, including key skills and portfolios, and the final part looks at autonomous assessment (self- and peer).

CHAPTER 5

Doecke, B. (ed.) (1999) *Responding to Students' Writing*, Norwood, Australia: Australian Association for the Teaching of English.

An edited collection of papers which centre on the vexed question of 'how best to respond to students' writing?'. The focus of some of the papers is on 'creative' rather than 'academic' writing and includes response practices from across the school age range, as well as higher education. However, both the issues raised and the practical suggestions offered will be of interest to teachers of academic writing in higher education.

Higgins, R., Skelton, A. and Hartley, P. (2002) 'The conscientious consumer: reconsidering the role of assessment feedback in student learning', *Studies in Higher Education* 27(1): 53–64.

Higgins *et al.* report on a study of students' responses to feedback in business and humanities courses in two universities. The paper illustrates some of the problems students face in understanding feedback, and also acknowledges the difficulties lecturers face in articulating 'tacit knowledge' about what is valued in their subject areas. Like Ivanic *et al.*, Higgins *et al.* provide suggestions for improving feedback.

Ivanic, R., Clark, R. and Rimmershaw, R. (2000) 'What am I supposed to make of this? The messages conveyed to students by tutors' written comments', in M.R. Lea and B. Stierer (eds) *Student Writing in Higher Education: New Contexts*, Buckingham: The Society for Research into Higher Education and Open University Press.

In this paper, Ivanic *et al.* survey a range of comments on students' writing given by subject lecturers and EAP tutors in a British and a North African university. The paper is a good illustration of contrasting styles of feedback and the effects these may have on student writers. Ivanic *et al.* argue that, in their feedback, lecturers should be trying to 'build students' sense of membership of the academic community' (p. 61). They provide a number of specific suggestions for improving feedback.

CHAPTER 6

Salmon, G. (2000) *E-Moderating*, London: Kogan Page.

This book covers all aspects of moderating on-line computer conferencing for effective learning. Salmon advocates a five-stage model for setting up and running conferencing, and discusses the skills, qualities and training that moderators need. She covers student fears and ways of facilitating access for students with disabilities, and why conferences succeed or fail. The second half of the book provides research-based checklists for practitioners.

Electronic Plagiarism Detection Project

The Joint Information Systems Committee (JISC) (http://www.jisc.ac.uk/mle/plagiarism/) with the collaboration of five universities, is looking at student plagiarism from the Internet. The project is reviewing the available electronic detection software, with a view to improving institutional policy and practice regarding plagiarism, and the results are to be disseminated to universities in the UK in due course. A guide for university policy making, as well as for lecturers, drawing from the project is already available (Carroll and Appleton, 2001). This covers many aspects of plagiarism, recognising that it is not always deliberate and that we as teachers have a responsibility to consider how we might design assessment tasks to reduce collusion, and how we communicate our expectations to students. It lists some of the most obvious clues to plagiarised work, and makes recommendations to institutions in communicating their regulations to students and being explicit about what they mean.

On-line journals

The on-line journal *Computers and Composition* (http://corax.cwrl.utexas.edu/cac/) contains a wide range of articles on the use (and usefulness) of technology in the classroom and for learning and teaching more generally. Another source of information is the *Journal of Online Learning and Technology* (http://gsep.pepperdine.edu/~jolt/about. html). The *Journal of Interactive Media in Education* (http://www-jime.open.ac.uk/) has links to the full text of on-line publications in educational technology. The website emoderators.com (http://emoderators.com/) is also a good source of resources and articles about moderating electronic conferences and related issues, and contains links to Listserv sites, netiquette guides, discussion forums and bibliographies.

References

Anderson, J. and Poole, M. (1994) *Thesis and Assignment Writing*, 2nd edition, Brisbane: John Wiley and Sons.

Angelil-Carter, S. (ed.) (1998) *Access to Success. Literacy in Academic Contexts*, Cape Town: University of Cape Town Press.

Ball, C., Dice, L. and Bartholomae, D. (1990) 'Telling secrets: student readers and disciplinary authorities', in R. Beach and S. Hynds (eds) *Developing Discourse Practices in Adolescence and Adulthood* (Advances in Discourse Processes, 39), Norwood, NJ: Ablex, pp. 337–58.

Bazerman, C. and Russell, D. (1994) *Landmark Essays on Writing Across the Curriculum*, Davis, CA: Hermagoras Press.

Becher, T. and Trowler, P.R. (2001) *Academic Tribes and Territories*, 2nd edition, Buckingham: The Society for Research into Higher Education and Open University Press.

Berg, E.C. (2000) 'Preparing ESL students for Peer Response', *TESOL Journal* 8(2): 20–5.

Blackburn, R. and Jarman, J. (1993) 'Changing inequalities in access to British universities', *Oxford Review of Education* 19(2): 197–214.

Brandt, D. (1990) *Literacy as Involvement: The Acts of Writers, Readers and Texts*, Carbondale: Southern Illinois University Press.

Breen, R., Lindsay, R., Jenkins, A. and Smith, P. (2001) 'The role of information and communication technologies in a university learning environment', *Studies in Higher Education* 26(1): 95–114.

Brown, G., Bull, J. and Pendlebury, M. (1997) *Assessing Student Learning in Higher Education*, London: Routledge.

Brown, S. (1999) 'Assessing practice', in S. Brown and A. Glasner (eds) *Assessment Matters in Higher Education: Choosing and Using Diverse Approaches*, Buckingham: The Society for Research into Higher Education and Open University Press.

Brown, S. and Glasner, A. (eds) (1999) *Assessment Matters in Higher Education: Choosing and Using Diverse Approaches*, Buckingham: Society for Research into Higher Education and Open University Press.

Bruner, J. (1983) *Child's Talk: Learning to Use Language*, Oxford: Oxford University Press.

Buranen, L. (1999) '"But I wasn't cheating": plagiarism and cross-cultural mythology', in L. Buranen and A.M. Roy (eds) *Perspectives on Plagiarism and Intellectual Property in a Postmodern World*, New York: State University of New York Press.

Carroll, J. and Appleton, J. (2001) *Plagiarism: A Good Practice Guide*, Oxford Brookes University and JISC (http://www.jisc.ac.uk/pub01/brookes.pdf).

Chanock, K. (2000) 'Comments on essays: do students understand what tutors write?', *Teaching in Higher Education* 5(1): 95–105.

Clark, R., Cottey, A., Constantinou, C. and Yeoh, Don Chuan (1990) 'Rights and obligations in student writing', in C. Clark, N. Fairclough, R. Ivanic, N. McLeod, J. Thomas and P. Meara (eds) *Language and Power*. Papers from the 22nd annual meeting of the British Association of Applied Linguistics, CILT/BAAL.

Clough, P. (2000) *Plagiarism in Natural and Programming Languages: An Overview of Current Tools and Technologies*, Technical Report No. CS-00–05, Department of Computer Science, Sheffield University, UK.

Collins Cobuild English Dictionary (1995), London: HarperCollins.

Collins Cobuild English Guides 6: Homophones, (1995), London: HarperCollins.

Crème, P. and Lea, M.R. (1997) *Writing at University: A Guide for Students*, Buckingham: Open University Press.

Crème, P. and Lea, M.R. (1999) 'Student writing: challenging the myths', in P. Thompson (ed.) *Academic Writing Development in Higher Education: Perspectives, Explorations and Approaches*, Reading: CALS.

Crowley, S. (1999) *Composition in the University: Historical and Polemical Essays*, Pittsburgh: Pennsylvania University Press.

Curry, M.J. (1996) 'Teaching managerial communication to ESL and native-speaker undergraduates', *Business Communication Quarterly* 59(1): 27–35.

Delpit, L. (1995) *Other People's Children: Cultural Conflict in the Classroom*, New York: The New Press.

Dudley-Evans, T. (1985) *Writing Laboratory Reports*, Melbourne: Thomas Nelson.

Elbow, P. (1981) *Writing with Power: Techniques for Mastering the Writing Process*, New York: Oxford University Press.

Feez, S. (2001) 'Curriculum evolution in the Australian adult migrant English program', in D. Hall and A. Hewings (eds) *Innovation in English Language Teaching*, London: Routledge in association with the Macquarie University and the Open University.

Fulwiler, T. (1986) 'The argument for writing across the curriculum', in A. Young and T. Fulwiler (eds) *Writing Across the Disciplines: Research into Practice*, Portsmouth, NH: Heinemann.

Galbraith, D. and Rijlaarsdam, G. (1999) 'Effective strategies for the teaching and learning of writing', *Learning and Instruction* 9: 93–108.

Ganobcsik-Williams, L. (2001) 'Teaching writing at university: a survey of staff perspectives'. Paper presented at the conference, Teaching Writing in Higher Education: An International Symposium, University of Warwick, 27 March.

Garner, I. and Lillis, T. (forthcoming) *Teaching Academic Argument in Undergraduate Psychology: Developing a Heuristic Tool*. Proceedings from Writing Development in Higher Education Conference, 2001, University of Leicester.

Goldbort, R.C. (2001) 'Scientific writing as an art and as a science', *Journal of Environmental Health* 63(7): 22–6.

Goodman, S. (2002) *Plagiarism or Writing Problem? The Views of Tutors on a Distance-taught English Language Course*, Centre for Language and Communications Occasional Paper No. 70, Open University, UK.

Graal, M. and Clark, R. (eds) (2000) *Partnerships Across the Curriculum*. Proceedings of the 6th Annual Writing Development in Higher Education Conference, Leicester: University of Leicester.

Grubb, W.N. and Associates (1999) *Honored but Invisible: An Inside Look at Teaching in the Community College*, New York: Routledge.

Halliday, M.A.K. (1996) 'Literacy and linguistics: a functional perspective', in R. Hasan and G. Williams (eds) *Literacy in Society*, London: Longman.

Hay, I. (1996) *Communicating in Geography and the Environmental Sciences*, Melbourne: Oxford University Press.

HEFCE (2001) *Supply and Demand in Higher Education*. Consultation Paper 01/62, Bristol.

Hewings, M. (1999a) *Advanced Grammar in Use*, Cambridge: Cambridge University Press.

Hewings, M. (1999b) 'The academy meets the real world: response to audience in academic business writing', in M. Hewings and C. Nickerson (eds) *Business English: Research into Practice*, Harlow, UK: Longman in association with The British Council.

Higgins, R., Hartley, P. and Skelton, A. (2001) 'Getting the message across: the problem of communicating assessment feedback. Points for debate', *Teaching in Higher Education* 6(2): 269–74.

Higgins, R., Skelton, A. and Hartley, P. (2002) 'The conscientious consumer: reconsidering the role of assessment feedback in student learning', *Studies in Higher Education* 27(1): 53–64.

Hilgers, T.L., Hussey, E.L. and Stitt-Bergh, M. (1999) 'As you're writing, you have these epiphanies: what college students say about writing and learning in their majors', *Written Communication* 16(3): 317–53.

Horner, B. and Lu, Min-Zhan (1999) *Representing the 'Other': Basic Writers and the Teaching of Basic Writing*, Urban, IL: NCTE.

Hyland, K. (2000) *Disciplinary Discourses: Social Interactions in Academic Writing*, Harlow: Pearson Education Limited.

Ivanic, R. (1998) *Writing and Identity: The Discoursal Construction of Identity in Academic Writing*, Amsterdam: John Benjamins.

Ivanic, R., Clark, R. and Rimmershaw, R. (2000) 'What am I supposed to make of this? The messages conveyed to students by tutors' written comments', in M.R. Lea and B. Stierer (eds) *Student Writing in Higher Education: New Contexts,*

Buckingham: Society for Research into Higher Education and Open University Press.

Johns, T. and Dudley-Evans, T. (1981) 'A team-teaching approach to lecture comprehension for overseas students', in *The Teaching of Listening Comprehension*, ELT Documents Special, The British Council.

Knight, P.T. (ed.) (1995) *Assessment for Learning in Higher Education*, London: Kogan Page.

Lea, M.R. (2001) 'Computer conferencing and assessment: new ways of writing in higher education', *Studies in Higher Education* 26(2): 163–84.

Lea, M.R. and Street, B. (1998) 'Student writing in higher education: an academic literacies approach', *Studies in Higher Education* 23(2): 157–72.

Lea, M.R. and Street, B. (2000) 'Student writing and staff feedback in higher education: an academic literacies approach', in M.R. Lea and B. Stierer (eds) *Student Writing in Higher Education: New Contexts*, Buckingham: Society for Research into Higher Education and Open University Press.

Leki, I. (2001) *Academic Writing Programs*, Alexandria, VA: TESOL.

Lillis, T. (1996) 'Essay writing starter', in S. Drew and R. Bingham (eds) *Student Skills*, Aldershot: Gower.

Lillis, T. (1999) 'Whose "Common Sense?" Essayist literacy and the institutional practice of mystery', in C. Jones, J. Turner and B. Street (eds) *Students Writing in the University: Cultural and Epistemological Issues*, Amsterdam: Benjamins.

Lillis, T. (2001) *Student Writing. Access, Regulation, Desire*, London: Routledge.

Lillis, T. and Turner, J. (2001) 'Student writing in higher education: contemporary confusion, traditional concerns', *Teaching in Higher Education* 6(1): 57–68.

Longman Dictionary of Contemporary English (2001), Harlow: Longman.

Love, K. (1999) 'Unpacking arguments: the need for a metalanguage', in B. Doecke (ed.) *Responding to Student Writing*, Norwood, Australia: Australian Association for the Teaching of English.

MacDonald, S.P. (1994) *Professional Academic Writing in the Humanities and Social Sciences*, Carbondale and Edwardsville, IL: Southern Illinois University Press.

Martin, J.R. and Veel, R. (eds) (1998) *Reading Science: Critical and Functional Perspectives on Discourses of Science*, London: Routledge.

Mayor, B. and Swann, J. (2001) 'The English language and "global" teaching', in M.R. Lea and K. Nicoll (eds) *Distributed Learning: Social and Cultural Approaches to Practice*, London and New York: Routledge.

McKinney, C. and Swann, J. (2001) 'Developing a sociolinguistic voice? Students and linguistic descriptivism', *Journal of Sociolinguistics* 5(4): 576–90.

McNamara, D. and Harris, R. (eds) (1997) *Overseas Students in Higher Education: Issues in Teaching and Learning*, London: Routledge.

Murray, D. (1987) *Write to Learn*, New York: Holt, Rinehart and Winston.

National Committee of Inquiry into Higher Education (Dearing Report) (1997) *Higher Education in the Learning Society: Report of the National Committee*, London: HMSO.

New South Wales Board of Studies (1991) *1990 HSC Sample Answers, 2/3 Unit Modern History,* North Sydney, Australia: Board of Studies.

Open University (1996) B800 *Foundations of Senior Management,* Assignment Booklet, Milton Keynes: Open University.

Open University (2001) A210 *Approaching Literature,* Assignment Booklet, Milton Keynes: Open University.

Open University (2002a) U210/AB02 *The English Language: Past, Present and Future,* Assignment Booklet, Milton Keynes: Open University.

Open University (2002b) *E300 Assignment Book and Project Guide,* Milton Keynes: Open University.

Oxford Advanced Learner's Dictionary (2000), Oxford: Oxford University Press.

Pardoe, S. (1994) 'Learning to write in a new educational setting: a focus on the writer's purpose', Centre for Language in Social Life Working Paper No 58, Lancaster: Centre for Language in Social Life, University of Lancaster.

Payne, J. (1995) *Collins Cobuild English Guides 8: Spelling,* London: HarperCollins.

Pennycook, A. (1996) 'Borrowing others' words: text, ownership, memory, and plagiarism', *TESOL Quarterly* 30(2): 201–30.

Penz, M. and Shott, M. (1988) *Handling Experimental Data,* Milton Keynes: Open University Press.

Prior, P. (1998) *Writing/Disciplinarity: A Sociohistoric Account of Literate Activity in the Academy.* Mahwah, NJ: Erlbaum.

Quality Assurance Agency (May 2000) *Code of Practice for the Assurance of Academic Quality and Standards in Higher Education,* section 6: 'Assessment of students', Gloucester: Quality Assurance Agency. Http://www.qaa.ac.uk/public/cop/copaosfinal/genprin.htm#fsp

Ramsden, B. (2001) *Patterns of Higher Education Institutions in the UK,* Report of the Long-term Strategy Group of UUK, Bristol: HEFCE.

Reid, J. (1984) 'ESL composition: the linear product of American thought', *College Composition and Communication* 35(4): 449–52.

Reynolds, M. and Trehan, K. (2000) 'Assessment: a critical perspective', *Studies in Higher Education* 25(3): 267–78.

Richardson, J.T.E. (2000) *Researching Student Learning: Approaches to Studying in Computer-based and Distance Education.* Buckingham: Society for Research into Higher Education/Open University Press.

Rothery, J. (1996) 'Making changes: developing an educational linguistics', in R. Hasan and G. Williams (eds) *Literacy in Society,* Harlow: Addison Wesley Longman.

Salmon, G. (2000) *E-Moderating,* London: Kogan Page.

Schuller, T. (ed.) (1995) *The Changing University?* Buckingham: The Society for Research in Higher Education and Open University Press.

Shephard, K. (2001) 'Submission of student assignments on compact discs: exploring the use of audio, images and video in assessment and learning in higher education', *British Journal of Educational Technology* 32(2): 161–70.

Shields, R. (1999) 'Culture and the economy of cities', *European Urban and Regional Studies* 6(4): 303–11.

Stewart, S., and Richardson, B. (2000) 'Reflection and its place in the curriculum on an undergraduate course: should it be assessed?', *Assessment and Evaluation in Higher Education* 25(4): 369–79.

Storch, N. and Tapper, J. (2000) 'The focus of teacher and student concerns in discipline-specific writing by university students', *Higher Education Research and Development* 19(3): 337–55.

Swales, J. (1981) *Aspects of Article Introductions*, Birmingham: University of Aston (Aston ESP Research Reports 1).

Swales, J.M. and Feak, C.B. (1994) *Academic Writing for Graduate Students*, Ann Arbor: University of Michigan Press.

Swales, J.M. and Feak, C.B. (2000) *English in Today's Research World: A Writing Guide*, Ann Arbor: University of Michigan Press.

Swan, M. (1995) *Practical English Usage*, second edition, Oxford: Oxford University Press.

Tang, R. and John, S. (1999) 'The "I" in identity: exploring writer identity in student academic writing through the first person pronoun', *English for Specific Purposes* 18: S23–S39.

Thesen, L. (2001) 'Modes, literacies and power: a university case study', *Language and Education* 15(2/3): 132–45.

Toohey, S. (1999) *Designing Courses for Higher Education*, Buckingham: Society for Research into Higher Education and Open University Press.

Valiela, I. (2001) *Doing Science: Design, Analysis, and Communication of Scientific Research*, Oxford: Oxford University Press.

Vygotsky, L. (1978) *Mind in Society: The Development of Higher Psychological Processes*, Cambridge, MA: Harvard University Press.

Webster, F., Pepper, D. and Jenkins, A. (2000) 'Assessing the undergraduate dissertation', *Assessment and Evaluation in Higher Education* 25(1): 71–80.

Wertsch, J. (1991) *Voices of the Mind. A Sociocultural Approach to Mediated Action*, London: Harvester Wheatsheaf.

Wetherell, J. and Mullins, G. (1996) 'The use of student journals in problem-based learning, *Medical Education* 30: 105–11.

Wignell, P. (1998) 'Technicality and abstraction in social science', in J.R. Martin and R. Veel (eds) *Reading Science: Critical and Functional Perspectives on Discourses of Science*, London: Routledge.

Wray, A. (1996) 'The occurrence of "occurance"', in G.M. Blue and R. Mitchell (eds) *Language and Education*, Clevedon: Multilingual Matters.

Wray, A., Trott, K. and Bloomer, A. (1998) 'Plagiarism and how to avoid it', in A. Wray, K. Trott and A. Bloomer (eds) *Projects in Linguistics: A Practical Guide to Researching Language*, London: Arnold.

Young, G. (1999) 'Using portfolios for assessment in teacher preparation and health sciences', in S. Brown and A. Glasner (eds) *Assessment Matters in Higher Education: Choosing and Using Diverse Approaches*, Buckingham: The Society for Research into Higher Education and Open University Press.

Zamel, V. and Spack, R. (eds) (1998) *Negotiating Academic Literacies: Teaching and Learning Across Languages and Cultures*, Mahwah, NJ: Lawrence Erlbaum.

Zuengler, J. (1999) *Formality in Academic Writing*, course handout, Department of English, University of Wisconsin-Madison.

Index

Anderson, J. and Poole, M. 30
Angelil-Carter, S. 6
anthropology 45
applied disciplines: case study method
  67; and professional/academic
  duality 68–71; writing in 46, 66
argument 73; and academic writing
  26; for and against 25; building a
  case 59; challenge 60; conception
  of 25; different strategies 59;
  discussion 60; and epistemic
  conventions 27; exposition 59–60;
  functional stages 60; in history
  writing 59–63, 64–5, 66; in
  humanities/arts 48, 57;
  incorporating evidence into 61–4,
  64–5; knowledge of process 45;
  overall position 60; persuasive
  purpose 26–7, 58–9; rhetorical
  purpose 60; in social science 53,
  57; structure 59–61; taking a stance
  25; use of term 25
assessment: best fit strategy for 74;
  collaborative writing 86–7;
  contradictory expectations 73;
  criteria 77–80; dangers in
  participative 94–5; formative/
  summative distinction 76–7; for
  grading or teaching 76–7; guidance
  on 80–1; and identifying types of
  writing 81–9; and issue of power
  94–5; of journals/personal writing
  84–6; and non-traditional students
74–5; peer 93–4; and plagiarism
  95–9; portfolios 88–9; practices 2,
  16–17; preliminary issues 74–6;
  purposes of 75–6; requirements
  of assignments 83; self-assessment
  93, 96; strategies for 75, 100; and
  student feedback 125; students'
  participation in 92–3; tasks/text
  types 81–3; unforeseen outcomes
  of 76; wording/phrasing used in
  89–92; and writing in structured
  conferencing 151–3
assignments: commonly used terms
  90–1; initial question words 91,
  92; multimedia 155–6;
  requirements of 83; wording of
  89–92

Ball, C. et al. 71
Bazerman, C. and Russell, D. 7
Becher, T. and Trowler, P.R. 47
Berg, E.C. 40
Blackburn, R. and Jarman, J. 4
brainstorming 20, 35, 37
Brandt, D. 24
Breen, R. 137
Brown, G. et al. 76, 81, 82, 84, 96
Brown, S. 77, 84–6; and Glasner, A.
  81
Bruner, J. 12
Buranen, L. 99
business studies writing, two
  audiences for 67, 68

case study method 21, 81; functional
stages 68, 69; rhetorical purpose
67; structure 67
cheating 17, 96, 154, *see also*
plagiarism
Clark, R. *et al.* 127
Clough, P. 99, 155
collaborative writing 42–3; assessment
of 86–7; different forms of 6
communication skills 2–3; electronic
136, 141; and feedback 111–21;
synchronous/asynchronous 136;
written 141, *see also* feedback
computer conferencing: advantages/
benefits of 134, 145, 152–3; and
asking of open questions 144;
asynchronous communication 136;
cross-disciplinary 135–6; described
134; developing environment for
144–5; encouraging participation
in 146, 151; establishing ground
rules for 143; formality/informality
in 141, 144, 149; and fostering of
virtual community 141–2; ice-
breaking/awareness-raising
activities 137, 144, 148; influence
on writing for assessment 151–3;
language characteristics of 141–4;
move from social to academic
discussion 148–9, 151; and need
for clear conventions 153; practical
issues 136–7; and setting up
discipline-specific glossary 145;
strategies for developing academic
argument in 146–8, 149; structured
135–6, 141–53; sub-conferencing
135; synchronous communication
136; as written communication
141, *see also* electronic environment;
Internet; web sites
copyright 153
courses: dedicated 6–7; disciplinary
subject 7; study support/writing
centres 7; writing on-line 8–9

Crème, P. and Lea, M.R. 30, 44
Crowley, S. 5
curriculum: changes in 4; diverse
modes of delivery 4–5
Curry, M.J. 34

Delpit, L. 10
disciplinary writing 71; argumentation
in 59–61; categorisation 46–7; and
developing a stance on evidence 63,
64–5; and less endorsing/more
endorsing terms 63, 66; sciences/
humanities continuum 47–8; specific
register 54, 57; and understanding
of knowledge 48, *see also* applied
disciplines; humanities/arts writing;
science writing; social science writing
drafts 37–9
Dudley-Evans, T. 72

editing 41–2
Elbow, P. 33
electronic environment 8–9, 17, 156;
background 130–1; computer terms
132–3; and development of
academic writing 141–53; email 132;
Listserv 132, 157; map of resources
131; and multimedia assignments
155–6; and plagiarism 154–5;
referencing on-line publications,
conference messages, websites 153–
4; structured conferencing 135–6,
141–50,
151–3; word processing 131–2, *see
also* computer conferencing; Internet;
web sites
English for academic purposes (EAP)
108
English for speakers of other languages
(ESOL) 8
essay writing 3, 21, 22, 24; alternatives
to 81, 82; argument types 58–61;
concept 82; disciplinary expectations
45–7; diversity of 57, 82–3; in

humanities 57–61; plan 37; in social sciences 53, 57

feedback 17; ambiguity of keywords in 115; and assessment 74, 76; attention to 37–8; and clarity of focus/rationale 106–7, 128; communicating 111–21; complexity of 103; on content 105; cultural context 119; developing dialogues 121–2, 126; and discussions with other lecturers 128; effectiveness of 103, 128; electronic 112, 113, 121, 144; extended comment 126; formats 113–15; good 102; identifying purposes of 104–5, 128; individual/group 112; institutional demands 102–3; language of 115–19, 129; and lecturer/student relationship 118, 129; oral/face-to-face 103, 121; positive/negative balance 117; practice of 102, 121; presentation of 119–21, 129; principles 102–3; research on 103; spoken 112, 113, 121; strengths/limitations of structured proformas/open-ended comments 116, 117, 119, 122, 123–4; student comments 123–5; and student guidance 129; timing of 103, 128; understanding 101, 107, 129; usefulness of 101; written 102, 121
Feez, S. 44
freewriting 35–6
Fulwiler, T. 7

Galbraith, D. and Rijlaarsdam, G. 33
Ganobcsik-Williams, L. 2
Garner, I. and Lillis, T. 114
generative techniques 35, 37
geographical writing: as example of social science writing *see* social science writing

Goldbort, R.C. 49
Goodman, S. 95, 154
Graal, M. and Clark, R. 8
graphic representations 37; social sciences 53–4, 57; visual/numeric illustration/data 57
grammar *see* linguistic accuracy
Grubb, W.N. 6

Halliday, M.A.K. 149
Hay, I. 72
Hewings, M. 44
higher education (HE) 100; approaches to student writing 9–11; provision of writing instruction in 5–9; student writing in 2–5
Hilgers, T.L. *et al.* 2
history writing 67; argumentation in 59–63, 64–5, 66
Horner, B. and Lu, Min-Zhan 5
humanities/arts writing 46; based on argument 48; essay form 57–61; incorporating evidence 61–3, 64–5, 66
Hyland, K. 29

Institute for Learning and Teaching (ILT) 5
integrating the process approach and text analysis 43–4; building the context 43; independent construction 43; joint construction 43; modelling/deconstruction 43; teaching/learning cycle 43
Internet 16; course websites 134; downloading/using material from 96–7; electronic computer conferencing 134–7; evaluating information on 139–40; On-line Writing Laboratories (OWLs) 137–8; and plagiarism 154–5, *see also* computer conferencing;

electronic environment;
structured conferencing; web sites
investigative project report 23
Ivanic, R. 11, 74, 118; *et al.* 117, 120

Johns, T. and Dudley-Evans, T. 8
journals, assessment of 84–6;
collecting/responding to 36;
multiple functions/forms 36;
rhetorical purpose of 36–7

Knight, P.T. 81

laboratory reports 21, 24–5, 51;
alternatives to 81, 82
language: ambiguity in 115;
assessment problems 91–2; as
cultural toolkit for learning 11–
12; different uses of 110; for dual
readership 68–71; of electronic
conferencing 141–4; feedback
115–19; formal/informal 110;
key assignment words 90–1;
personal/impersonal styles 68–9,
110; and use of first-person
pronouns 69–70, 111; varied role
of 46
Lea, M.R. 145, 151, 152; and Street,
B. 25, 45, 71, 74, 118
Leki, I. 6
Lillis, T. 11, 33, 74, 100, 113
linguistic accuracy 13; apostrophe
32; complaints concerning 30;
grammar 13, 30, 31–2, 33, 107;
spelling 30–1
Love, K. 24

MacDonald, S.P. 47
McKinney, C. and Swann, J. 126
McNamara, D. and Harris, R. 75
marking criteria 77–80
Martin, J.R. and Veel, R. 6
Mayor, B. and Swann, J. 91, 119
metadiscourse 24

multimodal texts, social sciences 53–4
Murray, D. 34

On-line Writing laboratories (OWLs)
137–8
organisational techniques,
classificatory systems 56–7; essay
plan 37; list 37

Payne, J. 31
peer review 40–1, 93–4
Pennycook, A. 97, 154
Penz, M. and Shott, M. 51, 72
personal reflection *see* reflective
writing
plagiarism 16–17; acceptable
paraphrasing 99; avoiding
accidental 98; and citation/
referencing conventions 95, 99,
154–5; consequences of 95; dealing
with 97; electronic 154–5; and the
Internet 96–7; lecturer views on
95–6; pre-empting 95–9; and
unacceptable paraphrasing 98, *see
also* cheating
portfolios: assessment of 88–9;
described 88; strengths/weaknesses
of 88
prewriting techniques 34–5;
brainstorming 35; comparing
example texts 51; freewriting 35–6
Prior, P. 2
process approach 32–3; collaborative
writing 42–3; drafting 37–40;
editing/proof-reading 41–2; focus
of 33–4; iterative cycle 34, 37, 41;
journal writing 36–7; peer review
40–1; prewriting techniques 34–6;
reflection 41
project proposals 23, 47, 49–50, 67
project reports, in social sciences 53
proof-reading 41–2

Quality Assurance Agency (QAA) 102

Ramsden, B. 4
reflective writing 41; assessment of
    84–6
register 14; discipline-specific 54, 57;
    formality 28, 29; lexical items 28;
    personal voice 29–30
Reid, J. 22
report writing: diversity of 82–3;
    scientific 50–1
Reynolds, M. and Trehan, K. 92–3,
    95
rhetorical purpose 14; argument
    25–7, 60; case study method 67;
    implicit 25; journals 36–7; overt
    24–5; in social science 53
Richardson, J.T.E. 5
Rothery, J. 44

Salmon, G. 137, 143, 145, 153
scaffolding techniques 12; in feedback
    122, 126, 127
science writing 46; advice on reports
    50–1; example 52; functional stages
    of project proposal 49–50; pattern
    of 49; structured nature of 49;
    understanding conventions in 49;
    use of parallel texts 51
Shephard, K. 155
Shields, R. 26
social science writing 46; adapted
    from scientific method 48; and
    discipline-specific terminology 54,
    56–7; multimodal texts 53–4; and
    quantitative data 53; as science/
    humanities hybrid 53, 57; using a
    graph 55; and visual
    representations 53–4
spelling see linguistic accuracy
Stewart, S. and Richardson, B. 84
structured conferencing: described
    135–6; and writing for assessment
    151–3; writing as part of 141–50,
    see also computer conferencing;
    electronic environment; Internet;
    web sites

student writing: approaches to 9–11;
    assessment of 2; at centre of
    teaching/learning in HE 3;
    brainstorming 20; in changing HE
    context 2–5; classification of 20;
    commenting on 105–11; common
    errors 108–9; contexts for
    teaching/learning 5; conventions
    in 3; courses for 6–9; and entering
    particular disciplinary
    communities 2; handover point/
    taking responsibility for 127;
    helping to improve 19–20;
    introduction to 20; learning and 2;
    purposes of
    20–1; social aspects 10–11, 33;
    whole-class discussion on 20
students: assessment difficulties 74–5;
    and complex patterns of
    participation in HE 4; helping
    international 51, 75; increasing
    diversity of 3–4; increasing
    population of 3; participation in
    assessment 92–5
Swales, J.M. 48; and Feak, C.B. 44
Swan, M. 44

Tang, R. and John, S. 111
teaching approaches 16; integrating
    text/process 43–4; process 10,
    32–43; strategies 46; teaching and
    learning cycle 43; terminology 13–
    15; text-based 9–10, 21–32, 63;
    toolkit for 11–13; writing as social
    practice 10–11
text structure 14–15, 24; argument
    essays 59–61
text types 13, 16; and assessment
    strategy 81–3; differences
    according to discipline 45–7;
    register 14; rhetorical purpose 14;
    text structure 14–15;
    understanding of 21–4
Thesen, L. 6
Toohey, S. 82

toolkit approach: activities 13; defined
    12–13; heuristic 13; sociocultural
    learning 11–12
topic development 38–9

visual representation *see* graphic
    representations
Vygotsky, L. 12

web sites: addresses on 157;
    Bournemouth University 154;
    Copycatch 155; for courses 134;
    evaluation checklist 140; HE in
    South Africa 5; Indiana University
    at Bloomington 99; Internet
    Detective 139; and plagiarism 155;
    Purdue University 138; referencing
    of 154; Sheffield University 155;

University of California at
    Berkeley 139; University of
    Toronto 139; University of
    Wisconsin 140; University of
    Wolverhampton 89, 157, *see also*
    computer conferencing; electronic
    environment; Internet; structured
    conferencing
Wertsch, J. 11
Wetherell, J. and Mullins, G. 85
Wignell, P. 53
Williams, J. *et al.* 98
Wray, A. 31; *et al.* 98

Young, G. 88

Zamel, V. and Spack, R. 6
Zuengler, J. 29